Alphabet Smash

Christina Parker Brown

Published by EA Books Publishing a division of
Living Parables of Central Florida, Inc. a 501c3
EABooksPublishing.com

Visit Christina's Blog, http://akahomeschoolmom.com/alphabet-smash-freebies, (or purchase the Supplement) to claim your:

FREE *Alphabet Smash* Weekly Schedule Worksheet!

A schedule to plan every week as YOU want.

FREE Alphabet Clip Art Pages!

Fun colorful pictures for your child to cut and paste into their *Alphabet Smash* Notebook.

FREE Alphabet Block Letter Pages!

Big chunky letters for your child to decorate and put into their *Alphabet Smash* Notebook.

FREE Alphabet Bible Verse Copy Work!

For every letter of the alphabet, your child can copy God's word and keep in their *Alphabet Smash* Notebook.

FREE Alphabet Handwriting Pages!

For every letter of the alphabet, your child can practice handwriting daily and keep in their *Alphabet Smash* Notebook.

DEDICATION

This book is dedicated to my big brother, Harry A.V. Parker IV, who stretches me and believes in me.

I have learned it is those who challenge you most that teach you best.

ACKNOWLEDGMENTS

Always giving thanks to God, the Father, for everything,

Give thanks to the LORD, for he is good; his love endures forever. 1 Chronicles 16:34 (NIV)

I wish to personally thank the following people for their contributions to my inspiration and knowledge in creating this book:

- My husband, Richard Lee Brown, who provides for our family, so we can homeschool intentionally

- Friends who pray me through — Neecie, Beth, Allison, Lindy, and Donna

- Three beautiful girls, Jessica, Abigail, and Gabrielle, this is because of you . . . I will cherish our *Alphabet Smash* memories always.

CONTENTS

Dedication & Acknowledgements

Alphabet Smash Weekly Schedule Worksheet					
Week _____	Day 1	Day 2	Day 3	Day 4	Day 5
The Letter _____					
Pray					
Say letter sound(s)					
Kinesthetic letters					
Menu					
Field Trip/Errands					
Alphabet Book					
Handwriting					
Decorate Block Letters					
Cut & Paste Clip Art					
Bible					
Bible Readings					
Bible Memory Verse					
Character Trait					
Art					
Art					
Artist Study					
FUN Activities!					
Fun Activities!					
Fun Activities!					
Physical Activities					
Reading & Poetry					
Poetry					
Poet Study					
Mother Goose / Nursery Rhyme					
Read-aloud Books					
Academics — Math, Science, Social Studies					
Math					
Science					
Social Studies					
Careers / Vocations					
Audio — Visual: Music & Movies					
Composer Study					
Hymns					
Songs					
Movies To Watch					

Introduction

Cupcakes, Christopher Columbus, compassion, and crocodiles —what do all of these have in common? The letter C, along with caboodles of other things—including the ways that *Alphabet Smash* introduces your child to the letters of the alphabet and other endless fascinating wonders of the world.

Alphabet Smash is an easy step-by-step guide written for teachers to share and celebrate with children the many wonders God has blessed us with alphabetically. It provides a smorgasbord of opportunities and ideas for children to learn the alphabet. Designed as a 26-week curriculum, it can be used as a supplement or as a stand-alone curriculum for children ages 3 to 7 years.

By incorporating a letter of the week into all aspects of daily activities, children are able to consistently learn the letters and their sounds in everything they do in real life—including eating, errands, and entertainment. *Alphabet Smash* offers an integrated, organic approach to teaching children the alphabet.

This unit study of the alphabet creates lifelong memories with your child/children. It is engaging, flexible, and fun!

> The consideration of out-of-door life, in developing a method of education, comes second in order; because my object is to show that the chief function of the child—his business in the world during the first six or seven years of his life—is to find out all he can, about whatever comes under his notice, by means of his five senses; that he has an insatiable appetite for knowledge got in this way; and that, therefore, the endeavour of his parents should be to put him in the way of making acquaintance freely with Nature and natural objects; that, in fact, the intellectual education of the young child should lie in the free exercise of perceptive power, because the first stages of mental effort are marked by the extreme activity of this power; and the wisdom of the educator is to follow the lead of Nature in the evolution of the complete human being.
> ~Charlotte Mason (vol. 1 of Home Education, 96–97)

How Does It Work?

Every lesson covers one letter of the alphabet, beginning with the letter A and continuing on through Z, for 26 weeks. Each week your child will focus on a letter of the alphabet, learning its sound(s), and how to write it. Then the instructor may choose from a variety of options that integrate the letter with academics and the arts. Lessons provide suggested activities in over a dozen main categories with the following symbols, to help you find what you are looking for quickly.

Aa   Handwriting

Food   Science

Field Trips   Social Studies

Bible   Careers

Art   Books

Poetry   Music/Appreciation

Fun Activities   Hymns

Math   Songs

Movies

For every letter, the child will do suggested activities, incorporating them into daily life. It is not intended that every activity be undertaken, but those which appeal to the instructor and the child.

She might choose one or two that intrigues the student, another to target one of the teacher's goals for the child (like Scripture memory), one that is convenient, etc. The instructor has the freedom to decide to lengthen or shorten any lesson(s) by increasing or decreasing the number of activities to pursue for each letter. The letters can be completed in any order.

Children will make an *Alphabet Smash* Notebook as a portfolio of their accumulated knowledge and discoveries. As the child completes an activity, learning will be recorded and stored in the child's *Alphabet Smash* Notebook, providing the child with a keepsake that s he can proudly share with grandparents and friends.

Multi-sensory activities help serve up the delectable bits of knowledge to keep studies fresh and exciting every day. Even if you have children well beyond needing to learn the letters, they may also participate to soak in the host of exciting topics and yummy food covered in each lesson.

Why *Alphabet Smash*? Because it uses everyday situations to recognize letters, their sounds, and context in life. You have to eat, so why not eat foods that begin with the letter you are studying? As you listen to music, create art, and study character traits, your child will be enforcing the letter of the week and strengthening essential skills. But more than that, learning should be fun, *especially* in the early years. By smashing a letter, you learn it better!

Who uses *Alphabet Smash*? Moms, homeschool parents, Sunday School teachers—in short, any teacher looking to present the alphabet to a child children ages 3–7 using a flexible, fun, and creative approach. This curriculum is a letter recognition program, not a reading program.

What is "smash"? Smash is adapted from the "smash journal." Smash is loosely defined as: "sticking cool stuff in a book or journal." The *Alphabet Smash* Notebook that the child makes includes all the things she/he discovers and creates for each letter of the alphabet. The freedom lies in you and your child, utilizing as little or as many ideas as you consider practical.

My reason for writing and putting together *Alphabet Smash* is simple. Learning alongside our children is fun. It should not be drudgery. Colored pre-school workbooks have their place but don't increase the quality of our education. Learning alongside our children and learning together treat education as a way of life. And, as teachers, our goal is to point our children to God.

Getting Started

Copy the *Alphabet Smash* **Weekly Schedule** worksheet on Page 6 or print it FREE from http://akahomeschoolmom.com/alphabet-smash-freebies for each letter of the week. Plan ahead and fill in only the activities YOU want to pursue each week.

Alphabet Smash NoteBook

Have your child make their own *Alphabet Smash* Notebook. Let them pick out their favorite three-ring binder notebook or allow them to decorate a notebook with a see-through slip cover, so they can design their own cover. Allowing your child to take ownership, from the beginning, will get them engaged. I use Avery notebooks for just about everything. Purchase one that is at least 2–3 inches wide, so it will hold all the many things your child will do throughout the year. You can find these used at yard sales or inexpensively at Wal-Mart, Amazon, or other office stores.

The *Alphabet Smash* Notebook that your child creates becomes a portfolio that combines all things included in this book that you will do with your child or that she/he achieves independently. It is a wonderful keepsake of memories and can record what your child accomplished for the year. Make a new notebook each year.

Alphabet Smash offers many choices. Consider it like a smorgasbord and choose what works for you. Do not try to do it all. Some ideas you might use one year with one child and use different options with another child during another year. Some ideas were so easy and accessible that I did them with all three of my children for preschool and kindergarten. For some ideas, I waited until my children were a little older. Highlight ahead of time what you would like to do with your child and plan what you can use around your house to do it. You have the freedom to spend an additional week on a letter.

Get outside! Attempt to do as many of these ideas outside as you possibly can.

An environment-based education movement — at all levels of education — will help students realize that school isn't supposed to be a polite form of incarceration, but a portal to the wider world.
~ Richard Louv (Last Child in the Woods: Saving Our Children from Nature-Deficit Disorder)

As a new homeschool parent-instructor, I felt compelled to be inside. Traditional learning, I thought, was bound to a classroom—after all, that is where I learned. Now, after 15 years of homeschooling, I have realized just how vital it is to be outdoors.

Although many of these ideas have links and selections to watch on the computer and YouTube, don't neglect the idea that much of a preschooler's day should be outside. Academic lessons should be kept short, 10-15 minutes.

The sense of beauty comes from early contact with nature.
~ Charlotte Mason (vol. 1 and 2 of *Out-Of-Door Life for the Children*, 68)

Create a *nature journal* right away and allow your child to attempt drawing things out in nature from his or her observations. Any book with unlined pages will do. Furnish the child with colored pencils, crayons, or watercolors. Allow imperfection. You will see improvement as the year progresses.

As soon as he is able to keep it himself, a nature-diary is a source of delight to a child.
~ Charlotte Mason (vol. 1 and 2 of *Out-Of-Door Life for the Children*, 54)

Letter and Sound Reinforcement:

Sounds

Have your child sound out all of the previously learned letters' sounds (before starting a new week) in addition to the "new" letter of the week. It helps to have a list of letters on the wall. Learning all the sounds a letter makes is key to teaching your child to read.

Before doing any activity—art, music, food, field trip, or Bible idea, etc.—have your child say the letter, then the sound(s), and then repeat the word. For example, "We are going to the bank. B . . . B . . . bank."

Kinesthetic

We are what we repeatedly do. Excellence then is not an act, but a habit.
~ Aristotle

☐ Have your child form letters with his or her body.

☐ Incorporate sign language into learning the alphabet.

☐ Write the letter in both the upper and lower cases on top of each page of the *Alphabet Smash* Notebook. At first you will be doing all the work. Encourage your child to copy your letters. Every little reminder will reinforce learning.

☐ Use homemade play dough, or the real thing, to create upper and lower case letters. Create a letter with clay and help your child to copy your letter.

Recipe for Homemade Play dough
Ingredients:
1 cup baking soda
1/2 cup corn starch
3/4 cup water

Have your child mix the baking soda and corn starch in a pot, using the hands to break up any lumps. Add water. Put the pan on the stovetop over medium heat and stir constantly. Remove when mixture is incorporated. Have your child knead it into a smooth dough when it cools. Do not over-cook, or it will crumble.

☐ Use finger paints (store-bought or edible homemade) to write letters on paper or wax paper.

☐ Make your own upper and lower case letters on index cards. Play "letter concentration" by matching uppercase letters to their corresponding lower case letters.

☐ Find books at yard sales or used kids magazines for pictures to put on their alphabet pages in their notebooks. Cut large letters out of old magazines or discarded books.

☐ Observe letters when you travel on signs, license plates, and billboards. My kids would soon see a piece of string lying on the ground or purposefully chew a pretzel and exclaim, "Look, mom—an 'S'!"

☐ Cut letters out of sandpaper. Write letters in sand kept in a plastic shoe box or in a sandbox outside.

☐ Sort alphabet macaroni.

☐ Outside letters: Trace letters. Write letters in the dirt or use sticks, leaves, rocks, petals, pinecones, and other nature to create letters.

☐ Play the invisible letter game on your child's arm. Write the letter with your finger and see if your child can guess the letter. Try with capital letters only, lower case letters only, or both.

Try this while your child closes their eyes. Allow your child to write invisible letters on your arm, hand, or back too.

☐ Match upper and lower case magnetic letters.

☐ Using magnetic letters on your refrigerator or magnetic board, allow your child to place the letters in the correct order. Sort letters.

☐ Underline, with your child, the letter of the week in text from newspapers, magazines, or old books.

 ### Alphabet Book

• **Decorate Block Letters**: Glue items that begin with each letter onto large block letters as suggested in the curriculum. Keep these in the child's Alphabet Notebook for each letter. Go to http://akahomeschoolmom.com/alphabet-smash-freebies for FREE printable A–Z block letter pages or purchase the *Alphabet Smash Supplement*.

• **Clip Art Pages**: Teach children to cut out the clip art pictures from this book or in magazines or discarded books. Paste the clip art on the appropriate letter page (where the leading sound or letter from the image corresponds to the letter on the page). It doesn't have to be (and won't be) perfect. Let them take ownership of their work. I found it fun to get magazines like *Ranger Rick* or *National Geographic* and add pictures they find to their alphabet page. Once we even taped a preserved ant to the "A" page, traced and painted fingernails with real polish for the "F" page, and a put a lock of hair on the "H" page. Be creative. Go to http://akahomeschoolmom.com/alphabet-smash-freebies for FREE A–Z additional printable clip art pages.

Aa Handwriting Pages

Practice writing several upper and lower case letters every day. Be more concerned with quality instead of quantity. Better to spend 5 minutes on three perfect letters than 20 minutes on a sheet full of messy letters. I suggest, especially for pre-school, to practice copying three letters per day. For example, have your child copy three upper-case letter As on Monday, 3 lower-case letter As on Tuesday, and both upper- and lower-case As on Wednesday. Then see if the child can remember the letter of the week you are practicing to write on Thursday. Use the Handwriting Sheets offered in this program. Go to http://akahomeschoolmom.com/alphabet-smash-freebies for FREE printable handwriting or purchase the *Alphabet Smash Supplement*.

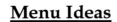

Menu Ideas

A week before beginning a letter, when you normally make your grocery list, look at the food ideas for the next letter, so you can have them prepared or purchased and can grab them easily from your pantry or refrigerator. Pick one a day or as many as you want. I encouraged my kids to try new things such as ugly fruit and kiwi, which they did not initially enjoy. Now, however, they eagerly try new things and are very fond of kiwi. *Use judgment on what your child can eat. Be very careful of choking with food and be aware of food allergies.*

Field Trip Ideas

Many of these ideas can be things you do in real life. Be aware and think about what you are doing, with what letter it begins, and verbalize it to your child. "Look, it is 'P' week, and we are going to the post office!"

Bible

Pray together every day.

Tell your child about the Bible story or idea mentioned. I highly recommend reading directly from the Bible rather than a watered down children's Bible. However, some children prefer to see pictures. You can find free printable coloring sheets of Bible stories online for your child to color as you read to them. Instruct them to narrate the story back to you in their own words.

The ABC Bible Verses for Memorization:
Unless noted otherwise, verses selected are taken from the King James Version. However, you can use any version that works best. If you change the version, keep in mind that it may change the beginning letter. You can download, for FREE, printable handwriting practice sheets of these Bible verses at http://akahomeschoolmom.com/alphabet-smash-freebies pages or purchase the *Alphabet Smash Supplement*.

Memorize a new Bible verse each week. Just five minutes each morning is enough to learn the verse by week's end. Memorizing scripture is a beautiful way to secure God's word in our hearts as well as our children's, and it also keeps it on the tips of our tongues. Short verses are best to begin with although I found my four-year-old was memorizing lengthy passages of poetry, scripture, and speeches if just given a chance. One of the longest pieces she memorized was the *Gettysburg Address* at the age of four. We just spent five to ten minutes a day, every weekday, practicing what we had learned and adding on a bit more. It truly is incredible what a four-year-old can do with memorization. You will learn alongside your child. Test each other. Have your child recite the piece in front of an audience of friends or family, or video it when it is mastered.

All children have it in them to recite; it is an imprisoned gift waiting to be delivered.
~ Charlotte Mason (vol. 1, part 7 of *Recitation*, 223)

Bible Ideas/Characters

The faults and strengths of Bible characters show believers how God can use anyone He chooses. The story of a Bible character can reveal history found in the Bible, and the story of the character can paint a picture of how God used that person. And how He can use us. Deliberately act these out or draw pictures to illustrate. Consider the Bible idea concept suggested and tell your child about it. Your child should be able to narrate several Bible stories by year end.

> But let the imaginations of children be stored with the pictures, their minds nourished upon the words, of the gradually unfolding story of the Scriptures, and they will come to look out upon a wide horizon within which persons and events take shape in their due place and due proportion. By degrees, they will see that the world is a stage whereon the goodness of God is continually striving with the willfulness of man; that some heroic men take sides with God; and that others, foolish and headstrong, oppose themselves to Him. The fire of enthusiasm will kindle in their breast, and the children, too, will take their side, without much exhortation, or any thought or talk of spiritual experience.
> ~ Charlotte Mason (vol. 1, part 5 of *Lessons As Instruments of Education*, 249)

Missionaries Learning about missionaries is an excellent way for children to see the big picture in terms of our faith. Attempt to show how the lives of these men and women can apply to their lives. Kids love stories. Focus on a missionary's story. YWAM Publishing and *Missionary Stories With The Millers* (Martin, Mildred A., and Edith Burkholder. *Missionary Stories with the Millers*, Minerva, OH: Green Pastures, 1993. Print.) are two good resources, and there is an abundance of information online for free. Google the particular missionary or search your library for these missionaries.

Copy Work Children should be able to copy words from a book or page. The *Alphabet Smash* Bible verse copy work and the A–Z letter pages are good practice.

Character Traits All of the character traits can be discussed on a pre-school level. Have the child use the word in a sentence and encourage them to try at least one character trait a week, such as *honesty* (in telling something that happened), being *helpful* (helping a neighbor rake leaves), or *thankful* (writing a thank-you note). Display the character traits, yourself, as well, such as *affectionate* (snuggle up with child), *giving* (give a gift to your child), or mention when you are *dependable* (when you drive your child to activity on time).

If you would like a free download of **Biblical Standards** that I created, go to www.AKAHomeschoolmom.com. The Biblical Standard Chart shows the offense or offensive behavior, the Bible verse or standard that speaks on the offense, and the positive character trait we are striving to emulate.

Art

Each week, display the artwork and projects that your child produces. Put as many of the art and activities, including pictures, into your child's *Alphabet Smash* Notebook under the appropriate letter. Be sure to date projects/artwork as your child completes it.

Handiwork: Real handiwork is the idea that children can make practical crafts that can be carried over into adult crafts, such as soap making or woodworking. It is okay if these crafts carry over into another week. Some may take weeks to complete. Don't divide handiwork skills between boys and girls. Knot tying is useful to girls, and sewing is a skill that both boys and girls can benefit from. All skills can be adapted for younger children. Sloppy work should not be allowed. Expect quality, not perfection, in their work. Real handiwork translates into useful life skills that can be made into presents and given to others.

Artist Study:
Put up as much artwork by an artist in your home or classroom as you can. Consider an easel to display it. Paintings can be found on calendars, or try www.artrenewal.com to download paintings and print them as 8X10s at your local office supply store. Ask for a teacher's discount. The bigger the picture, the better. Also consider going to museums to see the real thing. Many art museums offer discounted rates for students or free evenings. *Warning: Some paintings may be inappropriate for young children.*

Picture Study with Narration: To truly study a picture, ask your child questions about it: the time of day, the story she/he thinks is happening, colors, expressions, or background. Have them look at the picture for several minutes and then hide it. Encourage your child to narrate to you every single thing she/he remembers about the painting. Make it a game.

Picture Study with Photography: Try to act out the picture with your kids. My kids dressed in character for a study of Mary Cassatt and Norman Rockwell, and tried to mimic the paintings as closely as possible. In order for them to do this, they had to really study the paintings. I cherish the photographs I took of these studies. Check out my website at http://akahomeschoolmom.com/site/2010/picture-study-with-photography to see some examples of pictures we have taken.

Picture Study by Copying: Have your child attempt to copy the painting. I found my kids could be frustrated perfectionists and would not know where to begin. Try to focus on a small part of a picture. Attempt to paint or draw the picture yourself with your child. It is fun! My youngest child has really enjoyed using a light box to trace great works of art. This helped in not feeling so overwhelmed.

Poetry

To do a poetry study, read poems by your selected poet. It is important that children hear poetry read aloud. Poetry can breathe life into your schooling. Read an engaging biography about the poet as well. Have children memorize as least six poems a year. I recommend *Favorite Poems Old and New* by Helen Ferris. You can find many poems for each letter of the alphabet or look by author. Read poems together about nature, the seasons, holidays, and other topics. Occasionally assign a poem for recitation where both you and your child learn it and tell it to an audience of your family or friends.

Poetry is the rhythmical creation of beauty in words.

~ Edgar Allan Poe

Activities

Google activities you want to share with your child or purchase the *Alphabet Smash* ebook that include hundreds of links. **Together:** Do these activities together as much as possible. Have fun with this. You only have your kids for such a short time. The activities you do together make lifelong memories. My oldest children still have memories of our *Alphabet Smash* activities.

The most important goal is that you both (or all) enjoy the process. I involved my whole family with the letter of the week. My older kids looked forward to the special foods and activities, and would often join in the fun. Since I used this curriculum with each of my girls, they would usually mention, "Oh! I remember when we did this, Mom!" Or if I added something new, they would complain, "Gosh, Mom, we didn't get to do that!" It was a wonderful time we shared together. Check out my *Alphabet Smash* Pinterest Board at http://www.pinterest.com/christinabean1/alphabet-smash for visual ideas.

Life Skills: Many of the activities listed are life skills such as first aid, cleaning, and cooking. Learning how to shut a drawer correctly may seem silly, but teaching respect for doors and drawers at an early age can make a difference when children move to the teenage years. Try to accomplish as many of these as you can. When children are young, they want to do what you are doing, so take advantage of their interest.

Math Ideas

At this age, the idea is not mastery but exposure, or an informal familiarity with terms. If there is a way to show or give hands-on examples, do it. If any of these ideas are overwhelming or cause stress, then move on.

Science Ideas

Science is happening to our children every day. Taking time to notice and be aware is key. I highly recommend the book, *Mudpies to Magnets: A Preschool Science Curriculum*

(Williams, Robert A., and Robert E. Rockwell. *Mudpies to Magnets*. First ed. N.p.: Gryphon House, 1987.) and More *Mudpies to Magnets* (Sherwood, Elizabeth A., Robert A. Williams, and Robert E. Rockwell. More *Mudpies to Magnets: Science for Young Children*. Mt. Rainier, MD: Gryphon House, 1990. Print.). It is age-appropriate, and kids love the fun ideas and experiments. *Remember to try as many of these ideas as possible* outside *during the day.*

Social Studies Ideas

Social studies should build the child's awareness of self, home, family, and community.

Careers/Vocations:
An excellent website for further study is http://www.careerkids.com/careers/index.html. Here, when you can click on each career, it gives a description, working conditions, salary, education/training, job outlook, and additional resources. Some even have videos. To truly get an idea of what someone does on a job, have that person speak to your child directly.

Books

I suggest using *Five In A Row* (Lambert, Jane C. *Five in a Row*. Grandview, MO: Five in a Row, 1997. Print.) as a supplement to reading the books recommended for each letter aloud, as they have insightful activities and ideas to include as you share these stories with your child. I also used some living book (high quality, rich, literary classic books) titles from *Sonlight* curriculum (www.sonlight.com). Try to reserve all the recommended books online at your local library a week or so before each letter. In fact, for all books recommended, try to get these at your local library first, for free. Don't be afraid to read longer, richer, living books to your children.

When I began to homeschool, I thought my children had to be attentive to me to listen and ingest what I read. I have found, especially through one of my children who could not sit still, that it is okay to keep their hands or bodies busy as long as it does not disturb the reading. My middle child quietly stood on her head or quietly colored while I read. I highly recommend handicrafts as your children get older. Sometimes I have found books on CD, and we all would work on handicrafts while listening to rich stories and living books. We have truly enjoyed this time together. My kids are always disappointed when our reading/handicraft time is over.

To ensure your child has comprehended what you read, have them narrate it to you without interruption. Narration is simply telling back what they just heard in their own words. Try doing this with small chunks, say paragraphs or pages, initially. As their narration abilities improve, have them narrate after longer readings.

As knowledge is not assimilated until it is reproduced, children should "tell back" after a single reading or hearing: or should write on some part of what they have read.
~ Charlotte Mason (vol. 6, chapter 10 of *The Curriculum*, 155)

Be sure to look at the book list for each letter, a week or two before, and place books on hold at your library, so you will have them in time.

Music Appreciation

Composers: If there is one thing to take away from this section, it is to play music as you live your life. Listen to music when you are at home, when doing other activities, when doing nothing, or when driving in the car. Play one composer as background music for a period of time. Ideally do 2–3 composers in a 12-week term even if these overlap into another letter of the week.

Find "best of" CDs at your local library. For younger children, focus on the composer's childhood, as this is the part they identify with and will most remember and enjoy.

Classical Kids is also a great way to learn about a composer. Internationally-acclaimed stories bring composers and their music alive. Some of these are available at your local library. I suggest owning them. They are truly keepers.

Use "Classics for Kids" http://www.classicsforkids.com to listen to multiple composers. For many of these, you can click "Hear The Music" and listen just through clicking. Most of these composers can also be found free through the library or you can Google each on YouTube to listen. It is best to have a CD that you can play over and over.

Try playing music as your child creates art projects. Also try www.pandora.com or www.spotify.com to listen for free.

Host a birthday party for the composer. Celebrate with music, food of the times, and balloons. It doesn't have to be on the exact date. Have fun with it.

Hymns: I found a great resource on www.popularhymns.com. It provides not only the lyrics to the hymn but the story behind it as well. I just googled the hymn name on YouTube and found many renditions. Either way, make this a fun time with your child. You may find you recognize these same hymns in church!

Expose your children to the sheet music or preferably to a hymnal. It is important to show the music and not just the words. Choose hymns that glorify the Lord and engage the mind and the heart. There is one hymn for each letter but if you would like more, do more. The website link provides the most popular hymns by letter.

Songs: If you are unable to figure out the tune, just Google each song for videos. I picked popular songs that are easy to find. In most cases, there is a link for the lyrics. Sing these in the car or sing in the kitchen while you make dinner. Ideally, learn a song in another language. These should be fun!

Movies

This will be a fun part of your week. Please use discretion. Although most movies I recommended are rated G, some movies are rated PG and some may be too scary depending on your child; use your judgment. Pick one a week and snuggle up on the couch, pop some popcorn, and watch together. I treasure movie nights with my kids.

Try to get these from your library for free or ask friends if you can borrow them. We had many of these already in our movie library when the kids were small. You can also try kids consignment or thrift stores. Buy a used VCR and obtain VHS movies for 50 cents or less.

Use the movie time as a reward for doing well. Don't forget the popcorn!

Ideally, take your children to live shows such as plays at a local community college or theater. This is difficult to plan in conjunction with your alphabet study but will enhance the education experience. Each child can have a theater book in which you save every playbill. It is a collection of memories.

<u>Disclaimers</u>

Links to Third-Party Web Sites: If any links do not work, try googling words that are linked or suggested. Web sites contain links to third-party sites. These links are provided solely as a convenience to you and not as an endorsement by Christina Brown and *Alphabet Smash* to the contents of such third-party web sites. Christina Brown is neither responsible for the content of any third-party website, nor does she make any representation or warranty of any kind regarding any third-party website including without limitation (i) any representation or warranty regarding the legality, accuracy, reliability, completeness, timeliness, suitability of any content on any third-party web site; (ii) any representation or warranty regarding the merchantability or fitness for a particular purpose of any material, content, software, goods, or services located at or made available through such third-party websites; or (iii) any representation or warranty that the operation of the third-party websites will be uninterrupted or error free, that defects or errors in such third-party websites will be corrected or that such third-party websites will be free from viruses or other harmful components.

There may be some advertisements or comments on some of these sites that are inappropriate for young children. Please use discretion when on-line and always be in control of the computer when on-line with your child.

I do not endorse any of the ads on any of the links included. I spent hours finding what I thought were some of the best representations of examples for each activity, but I cannot control a company, a website's position, advertisements, or comments that are included on a website.

Some of the YouTube video links included may be too mature for a child, so be sure to watch them first before sharing. One example, for "X" week, is the eXplosion video link. While fascinating to watch, it may be troubling for some young children. Use your discernment. You know your child best.

Be careful of any activities, foods, or ideas that suggest using small pieces that could potentially be a choking hazard.

*If you have any ideas for this book, email me at chris@akahomeschoolmom.com

Let the
Alphabet Smash
begin!

The Letter A

 Sound /a/, /A/ , /ah/ (apple, ace, father)

 Kinesthetic: Form letters out of play-dough, your body, or make letters outside from nature (sticks, leaves, petals, pinecones, etc.).

 Alphabet Notebook
• **Block Letter Pages:** Draw an ant (three circles and six legs) or apples on your block letter **A**'s page.

• **Clip Art Pages:** Cut and paste clip art onto your **A**'s page.

Handwriting Pages: Practice several upper and lower case letters every day this week.

 Menu Ideas: **A**cai berry, **a**lmonds, **A**lphabet Soup™, **A**lphabits™ cereal, **A**lmond Joy™, **a**mbrosia, **a**nchovies, **a**ngel food cake, **a**ngel hair pasta, **A**nimal Crackers™, **a**nts on a log (celery with peanut butter and chocolate chips or raisins on top), **A**merican cheese, **a**pple (get one in every color and type), **a**pple fritters, **A**pple Jacks™ cereal, **a**pple juice, **a**pple sauce, **a**pple tarts, **a**pricots (fresh or dried), **a**rtichokes, **A**siago cheese, **a**sparagus, **a**vocados

 Field Trip Ideas: Go to an **a**irport and watch planes take off. Visit an **a**nimal shelter, **a**pple orchard, **a**quarium, **a**romatherapy shop, **a**rt gallery, **a**viary, or **a**viation museum.

 Bible Ideas:
Aaron, **A**braham, **A**bigail, **A**bsalom, **A**cts, **A**hab, **A**mos, **A**ndrew, the story of **A**dam and Eve, **a**ngels of the Bible

• **Missionaries:** **A**doniram Judson (1788–1850), Burma; **A**my Carmichael (1867–1951), India

Copy Work & Memory Verse: "All have sinned and come short of the glory of God" (Romans 3:23).

Character Traits: Accountable, affectionate, ambitious, appreciative, attentive

Art:
- Find free applique for kids patterns and instructions online.
- Fold an accordion out of a piece of paper.
- Create angels with handprint wings and an upside down handprint for the body.
- Make aluminum sculptures out of aluminum foil.
- Create animal masks using paper plates with two holes for eyes and popsicles sticks or tongue depressors for a handle.
- Draw or trace a Chinese aster.

Artist Study: John James Audubon, the West Indian American illustrator. Pretend to be John Audubon and draw things in nature.

Poetry:

Mother Goose:
AS I WAS GOING ALONG
    As I was going along, along,
A-singing a comical song, song, song,
The lane that I went was so long, long, long,
And the song that I sang was so long, long, long,
And so I went singing along.

Activities:
- Play animal charades. (Learn about an albatross or abalone.)
- Aromatherapy: Smell essential oils.
- Teach something simple in auto mechanics like how to check a car's oil level.
- Pretend to be an airplane.
- Look at an atlas.
- Teach child abdominal crunches.
- Act out a Bible story.
- Wake child to an alarm clock one morning.
- Discuss favorite actors and actresses and what they do.
- Go to an auction.
- Explain adoption.
- Teach how to be angry but not sin.
- Watch an astronaut in outer space on YouTube. Watch astronauts eat and drink and perform daily activities in space.
- Watch an acrobat.

- Teach your child to **ask** questions.
- Write (or draw a picture) to someone in the **A**rmy or the **A**ir Force.
- Watch an **a**erobics exercise tape and follow along.
- Be **a**ffectionate.
- Cut out an **a**dvertisement for your *Alphabet Smash* Notebook. Teach briefly what **a**dvertising is and how it works.
- Play the **a**lligator game: Put couch cushions or pillows in a circle around room. *Rule:* You cannot touch the floor or the alligator will get you. My kids LOVED this game.
- Say something to someone else about how **A**MAZING your child is.
- Go play at an **a**rcade.
- Learn the "**A**lphabet Song."
- Put **a**loe on a cut.
- Go on an **a**dventure.

Math Ideas:
- **A**dd on an **a**bacus.
- Draw an **a**cute angle. Find **a**ngles in everyday objects and around your home.
- Make an **a**rc using a compass (with parental supervision).
- Define: "**a**.m." means morning.
- Define **a**rithmetic.

Science Ideas:
- Study **a**stronomy.
- Read about **a**lligators. Watch **a**lligators in the wild online.
- **A**erodynamics (Explain with paper **a**irplanes that fly and those that don't.)
- **A**mphibians (Go to the pet store and see up close.)
- Read what the Bible says about **a**nts.

Social Studies Ideas:
- Find **A**frica, **A**sia, **A**ustralia, the two **A**mericas, and **A**ntarctica on map or globe.
- Learn about **A**ustralia. Make some **A**ustralian recipes.
- Learn about **A**pache Indians.
- Learn about **A**ncient History.
- Color a map of **A**merica.
- Learn what **A**.D. means in history.

Vocations: **A**ccountant, actor, actress, acupuncturist, agriculturist, air force, air traffic controller, ambulance driver, animator, archeologist, architect, army, artist, astronaut, astronomer, athlete, athletic trainer, auctioneer, automotive mechanic

Books:
- *Ten Apples up on Top!* by Dr. Seuss
- *How To Make an Apple Pie and See the World* by Marjorie Priceman

- *Angus Lost* by Marjorie Flack
- *Ask Mr. Bear* by Marjorie Flack
- *The ABC Bunny* by Wanda Gag
- *Animals, Animals* by Eric Carle
- *Alexander and the Terrible, Horrible, No Good, Very Bad Day* by Judith Viorst

 Music Appreciation:
- **Acoustic** music
- Listen to **A** cappella—(two words, two "Ps", two "Ls.") singing without instruments. Be sure to mention there is no music, only voices.
- The **Andrew** Sisters

 Composers:

- John **Adams** 1947; Isaac **Albéniz** 1860–1909; Tomaso **Albinoni** 1671–1751

Listen to **A** cappella—(two words, two "Ps", two "Ls.") singing without instruments. Be sure to mention there is no music, only voices.
- The Andrew Sisters

 Hymn: "**A**mazing Grace"
"; "**A**corn Brown"

 **Songs:** "**A**nts Go Marching

Movies to Watch: *Alice In Wonderland, An American Tail, Anastasia, Annie, The Aristocrats, Around the World in 80 Days, Anne of Green Gables*

The Letter B

 Sound : /b/ (boy)

 Kinesthetic: Form letters out of play-dough, your body, or make letters outside from nature (sticks, leaves, petals, pinecones, etc.).

 Alphabet Notebook
• **Block Letter Pages:** Glue **b**uttons (can purchase at a craft store) or **b**eans onto your block letter **B**'s page. Or color the **B**'s **b**lack and **b**lue.

• **Clip Art Pages:** Cut and paste clip art onto your **B**'s page.

B b **Handwriting Pages:** Practice several upper and lower case letters every day this week.

 Menu Ideas: **B**acon, **b**agel, **b**aked **b**eans, **b**aked potatoes, **b**aklava, **b**alsamic dressing, **b**anana, **b**anana **b**read, **b**anana cream pie, **b**anana split, **b**arbecue, **b**arley, **b**asmati rice, **b**eans (**b**lack **b**eans or any variety), **b**eef jerky, **b**eef stew, **b**eets, **b**ell pepper, **b**erries, **B**ing cherries, **b**iscuits, **b**lack **b**erries, **b**lack-eyed peas, **b**lack forest cake, **b**lack licorice, **b**lueberries, **b**lue cheese, **b**ologna, **B**oston clam chowder, **b**oysenberry, **b**read, **B**rie cheese, **b**rownie, **b**roccoli, **b**russels sprouts, **B**ugels™, **b**ulgur, **b**un, **B**undt cake, **b**urrito, **b**utter, **b**utter cookies, **b**utter nut squash, **b**utter scotch

 Field Trip Ideas: **B**akery; **b**alloon festival; **b**ank; **b**arber, **B**askin Robbins™; historic **b**attle site (watch a **b**attle reenactment); **b**each; meet a **b**eekeeper; **b**ird sanctuary; **b**ook store (new or used); **b**otanical garden; **b**owling; ride a city **b**us.

 Bible Ideas:
Story of the Tower of **B**abel, tell about the **B**ible, the story of the **b**lind man, **b**ooks of the **B**ible, **B**alaam,

Barnabas, **B**artholomew, **B**artimaeus, **B**eatitudes, **B**elshazzar, **B**enjamin, **B**ethlehem, **B**oaz

• **Missionary: B**rother Andrew (1928), Eastern Europe

Copy Work & Memory Verse: "**B**elieve on the Lord Jesus Christ, and thou shalt be saved..." (Acts 16:31).

Character Traits: Brave, **b**old

Art:
• Try **b**asket weaving.
• **B**lottos: Fold a piece of paper in half and paint one side of it. Refold it and smoosh it together. When you open it, the paint image appears symmetrical on both sides of paper.

• **B**leach designs: Using bleach and an eye dropper, create designs on scraps of fabric or denim (adult supervision required).
• Coffee filter **b**utterflies: Paint coffee filters with watercolor paints. Colors bleed. Let dry. Attach clothespin or pipe cleaner for body, string, and hang. Can be used for Christmas ornaments.
• Make a necklace, **b**racelet, or key chain out of **b**eads.
• Try **b**eading with a kit or a package of **b**eads.

Artist Study: Bruegel the Elder, Pieter

Poetry:
Read Robert **B**rowning's poems online or in a book.
"The Pied Piper of Hamelin" by Robert **B**rowning
Poetry For Young People by Robert Browning and Eileen Gillooly

Mother Goose:
BAA, **B**AA, **B**LACK SHEEP

Baa, **b**aa, **b**lack sheep,
Have you any wool?
Yes, marry, have I,
Three bags full;

One for my master,
One for my dame,
But none for the little **b**oy
Who cries in the lane

Activities:
- **B**ounce a **b**asketball. Play **b**asketball.
- Toss a **b**each **b**all.
- **B**low **b**ubbles.
- **B**ubble **b**lowout: Put dish soap in a cup of water. Give child a straw and have them **b**low **b**ubbles until **b**ubbles grow out of cup onto table. Have child clean table when done (see picture).
- Make **b**utter: Fill clean jar halfway with heavy whipping cream. Add 1 or 2 clean marbles. Shake until consistency is as thick as butter. Take turns shaking. You can add a bit of salt to taste. Spread on warm fresh (banana) **b**read.
- **B**e **b**lind: Pretend child is **b**lind (use **b**lindfold) and have child eat one meal or walk the house (with your help) without sight (creates great discussions and memories).
- Hold a **b**aby.
- Buy a **b**ackpack.
- Get a **b**abysitter for child.
- Use a **B**and-aid™ on a **b**oo-**b**oo.
- Ride your **b**ike.

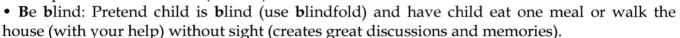

- **B**alance **b**eam walking; can use masking tape for **b**eam.
- Use **b**inoculars and watch **b**irds. Read about your state **b**ird.
- **B**uy **b**ird food for the **b**irds.
- **B**uild or put together a **b**irdhouse.
- Buy a **b**ird as a pet or visit one in a pet store.
- Purchase Mexican jumping **b**eans and explain what makes them jump.
- **B**low **b**alloons. **B**uy a **b**alloon from the dollar store.
- Pretend to be a **b**allerina. Rent a video or watch a real ballerina perform on YouTube or live.
- Have a **B**ackwards Day. Wear clothes **b**ackwards, eat dessert first, eat under table, etc.
- Distinguish **b**ig, **b**igger, **b**iggest. (Use stuffed animals.)
- Watch a **b**elly dancer perform.
- Find a picture of a **b**ody **b**uilder.
- Ask dad to grow a **b**eard, or draw a man with a beard.

- Make homemade **b**read.
- Grow **b**asil.
- Go **b**owling.
- Learn to **b**raid with real hair or 3 pieces of yarn on a clipboard or tied to something.
- Play with **b**locks. **B**uild something.
- **B**ounce child on your knee.
- **B**rush your child's hair.
- Pop the **b**ubbles in **b**ubble wrap. Kids love to stomp on these.

- Got a **b**ruise? Show it to your child or find one on them. (Best to look on shins.)
- Go to a **b**arber.
- Teach child to sew on a **b**utton (parent supervision required).
- Trace child's **b**ody onto butcher paper or blank newspaper roll; color clothes and make a face.
- Have a **b**arbecue.
- **B**ake something together.

Math Ideas:
- Count and sort **b**uttons by color and size.
- Make a simple **b**ar graph.
- Invest in **b**alance scales and allow child to measure different items around your house.
- Show how many zeros are in a **b**illion dollars ($1,000,000,000).

Science Ideas:
- Teach about **b**acteria, good and bad.
- **B**ats: Learn the different kinds and how many mosquitoes they can eat!
- See the life cycle of a **b**utterfly. Purchase caterpillars and watch their life cycles up close before releasing as butterflies (takes several weeks).
- Learn about the **b**rain.
- Read about **b**irds; **b**luejays. Watch a **b**aby **b**ird develop.
- Distinguish between several **b**irds in your area by their **b**ird call or song.
- Print free, printable **b**ird coloring pages online and color the major species that live in your area. Encourage child to identify birds in the yard.
- Catch **b**ugs in a **b**ug **b**ox and observe.

Social Studies Ideas:
- Learn about **B**enjamin Franklin or **B**etsy Ross.
- Learn what **B**.C. means in history.
- Explain and define a **b**iography.
- Discuss the **B**ill of Rights.
- Discuss the 3 **b**ranches of government. Simply describe what each branch does: Legislative makes laws, Executive carries out laws, and Judicial evaluates laws.
- Teach what **B**raille is and show your child **B**raille on various objects in the community such as **b**athroom sign plates and sign plates in federal and state buildings. Let them feel it with their fingers.

Vocations: Baker, bank manager, bank teller, beautician, bee keeper, book keeper, bus driver

Books:
- *The Berenstains' B Book*
- *The Big Balloon Race* by Eleanor Coerr
- *Berlioz the Bear* by Jan Brett
- *Blaze and the Grey Spotted Pony* by C.W. Anderson
- *Blueberries for Sal* by Robert McCloskey
- *My Blue Boat* by Chris L. Demarest
- *Classic Tales of Brer Rabbit*

Music Appreciation:
- Blues, ballads, ballets, barbershop, baroque, bachata, beach music, Big Band

Composers:

- Johann Sebastian Bach 1685–1750, Ludwig Van Beethoven 1770–1827, Hector Berlioz 1803–1869, Leonard Bernstein 1918–1990, Johannes Brahms 1833–1897

Hymn: "Battle Hymn of The Republic"

Songs: "Baa Baa Black Sheep," "My Bonnie Lies Over The Ocean," "Baby Beluga" (Raffi)

Movies to Watch: *Bambi, Beauty and the Beast, Benji the Hunted, Bolt, Brother Bear, Big Hero 6, Brave, A Bug's Life*

The Letter C

 Sound : /k/, /s /(cat, city)

 Kinesthetic: Form letters out of play-dough, your body, or make letters outside from nature (sticks, leaves, petals, pinecones, etc.).

 Alphabet Notebook
• **Block Letter Pages:** Color with bright colored crayons, chalk, or glue cotton or confetti onto your block letter **C**'s page.

• **Clip Art Pages:** Cut and paste clip art onto your **C**'s page.

Cc **Handwriting Pages:** Practice several upper and lower case letters every day this week.

 Menu Ideas: Cabbage, cake, candy, candy cane, cantaloupe, carrots, cashews, cauliflower, celery, cereal, cheese, chicken, chicken pot pie, chocolate, cinnamon, cinnamon rolls, cocoa, coconut, coleslaw, cottage cheese, cookies, corn, corn bread, corn on the cob, crackers, cranberries, cranberry juice, croissant, cucumber, cupcakes

 Field Trip Ideas: Have a campout in the backyard. Visit campaign headquarters, a candy shop, or a carpenter. Go to a farm and see a cow calves; visit a castle; go to a cave cavern; visit a relative in a cemetery or go to a historic cemetery; tour city government offices; meet a computer programmer or a professional cook/chef; explore a corn maze; go on a courthouse tour; ride a carousel.

 Bible Ideas:
Story of and including the 10 Commandments, the Creation, Cain, Caiaphas, Caleb, Christ, Cleopas, Cornelius, Cyrus

Missionaries: Cameron Townsend (1896–1982), Central America; Corrie Ten Boom (1892–1983), Holland

Copy Work & Memory Verse: "Children, obey your parents in the Lord: for this is right" (Ephesians 6:1).

Character Traits: Calm, careful, caring, cheerful, compassionate, contentedness, cooperative, courageous

Art:
- Carve a bar of soap or block of wood (parental supervision).
- Sculpt something out of clay.
- Color driveway or chalkboard with chalk designs.
- Color with crayons.
- Make large crayon cookies by placing old, broken crayons into muffin tins, 2–3 colors per crayon cookie, baking at 300 degrees till melted (just a few minutes. You need to watch or it turns into a mess), let cool (can refrigerate), and pop out. Fun to give away.
- Stained glass crayons: Grate crayons between 2 pieces of wax paper, iron, and hang in window.
- Crayon wax resistance: Color picture on paper with crayons and then paint with watercolor or other washable paint. Crayons resist paint and show through in a beautiful way.
- Collage: Glue onto paper—buttons, fabric, noodles, leaves, magazine pictures, etc.
- Teach your child to crochet or find someone who can.
- Learn how to charcoal sketch.
- Cross-stitch with easy patterns and instructions online.
- Draw a caterpillar.

Artist Study: Mary Cassatt
Arrange yourself, family, and children into pictures similar to what she painted and take pictures to capture the memory. See Mary Cassatt picture study photographs on http://akahomeschoolmom.com/2010/picture-study-with-photography.

Poetry:
Read some of Lewis Carroll's poems
Poetry For Young People: Lewis Carroll by Lewis Carroll

Mother Goose:
COME OUT TO PLAY
Girls and boys, come out to play,
The moon doth shine as bright as day;
Leave your supper, and leave your sleep,
And come with your playfellows into the street.
Come with a whoop, come with a call,
Come with a good will or not at all.
Up the ladder and down the wall,
A half-penny roll will serve us all.

You find milk, and I'll find flour,
And we'll have a pudding in half an hour.

Activities:
• Make homemade confetti.
• Introduce calligraphy.
• Have a costume party. Or dress up for fun. Don't forget make-up too!
• Make crowns: Use cardboard for base. Add sequins, jewels, aluminum foil, construction paper, etc.
• Play copy cat.
• Pet a cat.
• Take a car ride.
• Play a computer game.
• Ride a carousel.
• Teach child to can fruits or vegetables.
• Pretend to be a cowboy or cowgirl.
• Cutting: Cut shapes, patterns, people animals out of magazines, etc.
• Cut fabric, sandpaper, ribbon, and plastic.
• Play cards (Go Fish, Old Maid, Crazy Eights).
• Play concentration.
• Peruse Little Contenders For The Faith Curriculum.
• Teach child to clean something (car, carpet).
• Crayon rubbings: Put coins, keys, leaves, paper shapes, grave stone, bricks, etc. under paper and, using long side of crayon, rub lightly until outlined image appears.
• Learn the color spectrum: ROYGBIV (red, orange, yellow, green, blue, indigo, and violet).
• Make a castle out of an old appliance box.
• Make a card house out of playing cards.
• Change colors of celery, Queen Anne's lace, or white carnations by leaving stem in water that is dyed with food coloring.
• Letter cookies: Make shapes out of refrigerated cookie dough and bake.
• Teach child to clear the table after a meal.
• Teach child to cook something by him/herself.
• Teach child to clean something such as tubs, toilets, mirrors, sinks, floors, etc.

Math Ideas:
• Introduce and make a calendar.
• Teach the colors. Play matching games with index cards (color each and name). Cut specific colors out of old magazines and make a collage of each color. Establish a color of the day and have everyone wear that color. Sort colored socks, blocks, beads, buttons, or rocks.
• Draw a clock face.
• Practice drawing circles.
• Explain clockwise and counterclockwise.

• Teach what **c**ircumference, **c**ylinder, and **c**ube mean. Show examples (lid, oatmeal **c**anister, and box).
• Let child push some buttons on a **c**alculator. Type in 07734 and turn **c**alculator upside down. It spells "hello." "Shell" is 77345. "Shoeless" is 55373045.
• Find a **c**ompass and help child figure out where north is located looking out of your house. Teach child all 4 points on the **c**ompass, which direction the sun rises (east), where the sun sets (west), and which direction a relative lives using the **c**ompass on a map.
• Explain how a **c**redit **c**ard is used and how it is not free money.

Science Ideas:
• Look for different types of **c**louds.
• Teach the meaning of **c**arnivore.
• Condensation: Fill Ziploc™ bag with 1/2–1 cup of water. Seal bag, tape to window, and watch **c**ondensation form on sides and top. Explain that **c**louds are made up of tiny drops of water like these.
• Colored water **c**hemistry: Using food coloring, make colors—red + blue = purple, blue + yellow=green, yellow + red=orange, and blue + red + yellow=yuck!
• Learn about **c**rocodiles.
• Study **c**limate. Use a rain gauge.
• Watch a **c**ockroach. "With regard to the horror which some children show of beetle, spider, worm, that is usually a trick picked up from grown-up people." ~ Charlotte Mason (Vol 1, II, *Out-Of-Door Life for The Children*, 58).
• Look at **c**onstellations; make a **c**onstellation with star stickers.
• Find pictures of **c**amouflage animals.

Social Studies Ideas:
• Learn about **C**hristopher **C**olumbus.
• Find out the **c**apital of your state.
• Explain the **C**onstitution briefly.
• Visit a **C**hinese restaurant.
• Buy **C**hinese food, egg rolls, fried rice, etc., and have a **C**hinese meal with **c**hopsticks.
• Visit a **C**uban restaurant.
• Locate **C**anada on a map.

Vocations: **C**ardiologist, **c**arpenter, **c**ashier, **c**hef/cook, **c**hemical engineer, **c**hemist, **c**ivil engineer, **c**oach, **c**ollege professor, **c**omputer programmer, **c**ounselor, **c**ourt reporter

Books:
• *The Very Hungry Caterpillar* by Eric Carle
• *Caps for Sale* by Esphyr Slobodkina
• *The Carrot Seed* by Ruth Krauss
• *The Clown of God* by Tomie DePaola

• *Corduroy* by Don Freeman
• *The Complete Adventures of Curious George*

Music Appreciation:
Christian, **C**hristian rock, **C**eltic, **C**ajun, **C**aribbean, **c**abaret, **c**alypso, **c**hoir music, **C**hristmas **c**arols, **c**ello playing

Composers: Frédéric **C**hopin 1810–1849, Aaron **C**opland 1900–1990

Hymn: "**C**rown Him With Many **C**rowns"

Songs: "**C**lementine"

Movies to Watch: *Cars, Charlotte's Web, Chicken Little, A Christmas Carol* (new and old versions), *Cinderella, Curious George*

Notes:

The Letter D

 Sound : /d/ (dog)

 Kinesthetic: Form letters out of play-dough, your body, or make letters outside from nature (sticks, leaves, petals, pinecones, etc.).

 Alphabet Notebook
• **Block Letter Pages:** Doodle on your **D**'s page. Using **d**ots from a 3-hole punch, glue **d**ots onto your block letter **D**'s page. Draw **d**rips on your **D**'s page.

• **Clip Art Pages:** Cut and paste clip art onto your **D**'s page.

D d **Handwriting Pages:** Practice several upper and lower case letters every day this week.

 Menu Ideas: **D**airy, **D**anish, **d**ark chocolate, **d**ates, **d**eep **d**ish pizza, **D**elmonico steak, **d**essert, **d**eviled crabs, **d**eviled eggs, **d**eviled ham, **D**ijon mustard, **d**ill pickles, **d**ip with veggies, **d**irty rice, **d**oughnuts, **D**oritos™, **d**ried fruits, **d**uck, **d**uck sauce, **d**umplings

 Field Trip Ideas: Visit a **d**airy farm, **d**eli, **d**entist office, **d**inosaur exhibit, or **d**octor's office. Take your **d**og to a **d**og park. Go to a **d**ry cleaners.

 Bible Ideas:
Daniel and the Lion's **D**en, **D**avid, **D**eborah, **D**elilah, **D**emetrius, **D**orcas

• **Missionaries:** **D**avid Livingstone (1813–1873), Africa; **D**.L. Moody (1837–1899), America

Copy Work & Memory Verse: "Depart from evil, and **d**o good..." (Psalm 34:14).

Character Traits: **D**aring, **d**ecisive, **d**elightful, **d**ependable, **d**etermined, **d**evoted, **d**isciplined, **d**iligent, **d**utiful

Art:
- Make a **d**ream catcher.
- Make a **d**oll.
- Build a cardboard **d**oll house and make miniature furniture to fill it.
- Trace a **d**inosaur.
- Make a **d**ragon.
- Make a **d**oor hanger for your room.

Artist Study: Edgar **D**egas

Poetry:
Read Emily **D**ickinson's poems online and on Ambleside's online Poems of Emily Dickinson
Poetry For Young People: Emily Dickinson by Frances Schoonmaker Bolin
Read **Dr. Seuss:** There is a plethora of books available. I recommend Dr. Seuss's *ABC*, *Green Eggs and Ham*, *Fox in Socks*, *Hop on Pop*, *The Cat in the Hat*.

Mother Goose:
DIDDLE **D**IDDLE **D**UMPLING
Diddle diddle dumpling, my son John
Went to bed with his breeches on,
One stocking off, and one stocking on;
Diddle diddle dumpling, my son John.

Activities:
- Make paper **d**olls.
- Play **d**ominos.
- Watch **d**ominos fall. Set **d**ominos up so that when you knock one over, they all fall over.
- Walk, bathe, pet, and feed a **d**og.
- Find and blow a **d**andelion (and make a wish).
- Play **d**arts (parent supervision).
- Draw a **d**ial pad on paper and teach child to **d**ial 911.
- Pick **d**aisies.
- Love your **d**addy (call him, **d**raw him a picture, and email or mail it to his work).
- Play with **d**olls. Have your child share her entire **d**ay with her **d**oll.
- Play **d**inosaurs; learn about a favorite **d**inosaur.

- Teach child how to shut a **d**oor or **d**rawer correctly. Teach not to slam. Practice.
- Play **d**uck, **d**uck, goose.
- **D**ance like no one is looking. Have child stand on your feet while **d**ancing. Pick up and **d**ance; **d**ip and spin. **D**ance silly.
- Play **d**octor using tissue paper and tape for bandages.
- Teach child to **d**ust and to use a **d**ustpan.
- Wash **d**ishes together.
- Show child how to **d**ribble a ball.
- Feed **d**ucks.

Math Ideas:
- **D**efine "**d**ozen."
- **D**imes; teach to count by 10.
- Point out a **d**ecimal point on a price sticker in the grocery store.
- Show and count **d**iamonds in a **d**eck of cards.
- Explain how something **d**ecreases.
- Roll **d**ice and add up numbers shown.
- Teach a **d**iagonal line.
- **D**ivide M&M'S™ between siblings; allow your child to try **d**ividing.

Science Ideas:
- Learn about **d**olphins; google the sound a **d**olphin makes. Learn about **d**onkeys or **d**inosaurs.
- **D**iscover **d**iffusion.
- **D**iscover **d**ensity.

Social Studies Ideas:
- Learn about **D**aniel Boone, **D**avy Crockett, or Frederick **D**ouglas.
- Briefly discuss the **D**eclaration of Independence; the **D**eclaration of the Congress of the Thirteen United States of America, on the 4th of July, 1776, that formally declared the colonies were free and independent states, not subject to the government of Great Britain.
- Learn about a **d**esert.

Vocations: **D**ancer, **d**entist, **d**ental hygienist, **d**ermatologist, **d**esigner, **d**etective, **d**ietician, **d**isc jockey, **d**octor, **d**og walker, **d**rafter

Books:
- *Go, Dog. Go! by P.D. Eastman*
- *Duncan the Dancing Duck by Syd Hoff*
- *Danny and the Dinosaur by Syd Hoff*
- *The Story of Dr. Dolittle by Hugh Lofting*
- *Dolphin Adventure by Wayne Grover*

• *Down, Down the Mountain by Ellis Credle*

Music Appreciation:
Disco

Composers: Claude Debussy 1862–1918, Paul Dukas 1865–1935, Antonin Dvorák 1841 –1904

Hymn: "Doxology"

Songs: "Hey Diddle Diddle," "The Farmer in the Dell," "How Much Is That Doggie?"

Movies to Watch: *Despicable Me, Despicable Me 2, Down Under, Dr. Suess, Dumbo*

Notes:

_____

_____

_____

_____

_____

_____

_____

_____

The Letter E

 Sound : /e/ , /E/ (elk, be)

 Kinesthetic: Form letters out of play-dough, your body, or make letters outside from nature (sticks, leaves, petals, pinecones, etc.).

 <u>Alphabet Notebook</u>
• **Block Letter Pages:** Glue on colored **e**gg shells. Mix 1/2 cup hot water, 1 Tbsp vinegar, and a few drops of food coloring. Put **e**gg shells in mix. Let dry and and glue onto your block letter E's page.

• **Clip Art Pages:** Cut and paste clip art onto your E's page.

Ee **Handwriting Pages:** Practice several upper and lower case letters every day this week.

 Menu Ideas: Earl Grey tea, **e**clair, **e**damame, **e**ggs (Benedict, deviled, fried, scrambled poached, soft boiled), **e**ggplant, **e**gg foo young, **e**ggplant parmigiana, **e**gg rolls, **e**lbow macaroni noodles, **e**lephant **e**ar pastry, Empire apples, **e**nchiladas, English muffins, **e**scargot, **e**skimo pies, **es**presso, **e**vaporated milk, Evian™ water

 Field Trip Ideas: Go to an **e**gg farm; meet an **e**lectrician; learn about **e**mergency services; or visit an **e**xotic pet shop.

 Bible Ideas:
Elijah, Elisabeth, Elisha, Ephraim, Esau, Esther, Eve, Ezekial, Ezra, the star in the East, **e**ternal life, the Exodus from Egypt

• **Missionaries:** Eric Liddell (1902–1945), China; Elisabeth Elliot (1926), Ecuador

Copy Work & Memory Verse: "Even a child is known by his actions" (Proverbs 20:11).

Character Traits: Eager, easy-going, encouraging, energetic, enthusiastic

Art:
- Eyedropper art: Using runny paint, take an eyedropper and drop paint splats from different heights.
- Learn the art of embroidery.
- Eggshell art: Crush the shells of several eggs and soak them in different cups of colored water using food coloring. Let dry on paper towel; then glue onto a drawn egg shape. Layer the colors and make designs.
- Egg yolk painting: Add paint to the yolks of eggs and brush onto paper with paintbrush. It makes the colors super shiny. Wash hands afterwards.
- Decorate Easter eggs.
- Paint on an easel.

Poetry:

Mother Goose:
ELIZABETH
Elizabeth, Elspeth, Betsy, and Bess,
They all went together to seek a bird's nest;
They found a bird's nest with five eggs in,
They all took one, and left four in.

Activities:
- Decorate an envelope.
- Wear earmuffs.
- Buy wear/earrings.
- Have an egg relay race with spoon (can use plastic eggs).
- Exercise.
- Learn about eagles and elephants.
- Use egg cartons to sort buttons, rocks, beans, etc.
- Make eggs using an egg beater.
- Try to kiss your elbow (smile).
- Send an email with your child.
- Give child an Eskimo kiss.
- Listen to a movie or book on CD with earphones.
- Listen to a song with earphones (not too loud).
- Ride in an elevator.
- Ride an escalator.
- Discuss eavesdropping.
- Discuss entrances and exits.
- Make a fire escape plan and meeting place in the event of a fire or emergency.
- Teach child to edify another child.

- Mail an envelope.
- Exhale.
- Teach child to empty the trash.
- Draw emotions on faces, include eyebrows (happy, sad, mad, surprised).
- Shade an area in pencil and then erase a design in it.
- Draw something in pencil and then erase it.

Math Ideas:
- Estimating: Estimate how many M&M's™ are in a jar.
- Show an equation.
- Draw an equilateral triangle.
- Explain even numbers using toys.

Science Ideas:
- Learn about elephants, eagles, and endangered and extinct species.
- Investigate earthquakes and erosion.
- Discover the benefits of exercise.
- What is the epidermis?
- Learn about Eskimos.
- Evaporation experiments with hand sanitizer, drinking cups, and clothes.
- Evaporation: Paint sidewalk driveway with water using large brushes. Watch it dry or come back later. Wait for wet hair to dry by evaporation.
- Make a sparkly explosion with baking soda, vinegar, and glitter.
- Electricity: Thomas Edison and the electric light bulb.
- Static Electricity: Take a balloon, rub against your shirt, and hold it on a wall. Observe how it sticks.
- Make an eruption with Diet Coke™ and Mentos™. Watch it on YouTube.

Social Studies Ideas:
- Thomas Edison, Albert Einstein
- Emigrants
- Learn about Egypt and Egyptians.
- Think of ways your child can earn money—chores, picking up sticks in the yard, etc.

Vocations: Ecologist, economist, editor, educator, electrical engineer, electrician, embalmer, emergency medical technician, engineer, engraver, evangelist, environmental scientist, exterminator, eye doctor

Books:
- *Eli* by Bill Peet
- *Eloise Wilkin Stories*
- *Elephant Families* by Arthur Dorros
- *The Little Engine That Could* by Watty Piper

- *The Empty Pot* by Demi
- *The Elves and the Shoemaker* (Fairy Tale)

 Music Appreciation:
Environmental (sounds) such as thunderstorms, ocean, forrest, etc., or elevator music

 Composers:
Edward Elgar 1857–1934

 Hymn: "Emmanuel, Emmanuel," "El Shaddai"

 Songs: "Everything Grows" (Raffi)

 Movies to Watch: *The Adventures of Elmo in Grouchland*, *Enchanted*, *Baby Einstein*, *Epic*

Notes:

The Letter F

 Sound : /f/ (fun)

 Kinesthetic: Form letters out of play-dough, your body, or make letters outside from nature (sticks, leaves, petals, pinecones, etc.).

 Alphabet Notebook
• **Block Letter Pages:** Glue feathers, pieces of fabric, or felt onto your block letter F's page.

• **Clip Art Pages:** Cut and paste clip art onto your F's page.

Handwriting Pages: Practice several upper and lower case letters every day this week.

 Menu Ideas: Falafel, Famous Amos cookies, Fanta™ (drink), fajita, fava beans, feta cheese, Fig Newtons™, fish (all kinds), fish sticks, flap jacks, flour, fortune cookies, frankfurters, Frappuccino™ (make your own with coffee ice-cream and chocolate ice-cream), French bread, French fries, French toast, French vanilla ice-cream, fried chicken, fried rice, frozen yogurt, fruit, fruit cake, fruit cocktail, fruit roll-ups, fruit salad, fudge, fudge popsicles, Fudge Shop Cookies™, fudge sundae, Fuji apples, funnel cakes, Funyuns™

 Field Trip Ideas: Go to a fabric shop, local factory, farm, farmer's market, fire station, fish hatchery, florist, or funeral home.

 Bible Ideas:
Fear (study read all the verses on fear), fishes, feeding of the five thousand, or the fish Peter pulled into the boat, Festus, frankincense

• **Missionary:** Florence Young (1856–1940), Solomon Islands, China

Copy Work & Memory Verse: "Fear not: for I am with thee" (Isaiah 43:5).

Character Traits: Fair, faithful, frank, friendly, focused, forgiving, friendly

Art:
- Color flowers.
- Learn the art of flower arranging.
- Create a butterfly with your child's footprints for wings.
- Trace child's feet (be sure to date paper).
- Redo a frame (get one used at a thrift store or yard sale. Paint it or sponge paint it, and decorate with buttons, shells, puzzle pieces, etc., and put in picture of child).
- Make fingerprint art by making fingerprints in ink and then adding arms, legs, and a face.
- Finger paint together.
- Have your child draw your family—dad, mom, brother, sister, and pet, etc.
- Make a friendship bracelet.

Poetry:

Mother Goose:
THE FARMER AND THE RAVEN
A farmer went trotting upon his gray mare,
Bumpety, bumpety, bump!
With his daughter behind him so rosy and fair,
Lumpety, lumpety, lump!

A raven cried croak! and they all tumbled down,
Bumpety, bumpety, bump!
The mare broke her knees, and the farmer his crown,
Lumpety, lumpety, lump!

The mischievous raven flew laughing away,
Bumpety, bumpety, bump!
And vowed he would serve them the same the next day,
Lumpety, lumpety lump!

Activities:
- Make a fan by folding paper accordion style. (Have child color a picture on it first.)
- Go fishing.
- Teach basic first aid.
- Put together a first aid kit.
- Have cheese fondue (dip bread and veggies) and chocolate fondue (dip fruit— bananas, pineapple, apples, etc.). You can use a double boiler and a fork; it doesn't have to be fancy.
- Dress up fancy.

- Feel different types of **f**abric (silk, satin, denim, **f**elt, cotton, polyester, wool, etc.).
- Make a **f**elt board (glue black **f**elt onto card board; any size you want). Make easy homemade **f**elt board games of **f**elt.
- Make or buy a **f**rustration pencil.
- **F**reeze some soda or juice in a cup.
- Go to a county **f**air.
- Discuss **f**eelings and draw each one—happy, sad, surprised, mad, etc.
- Make a **f**ire in a **f**ire pit or **f**ireplace (parent supervised).
- Pick or buy **f**lowers for your child to enjoy and put them on your kitchen table or their nightstand.
- Put a blanket on the ground and pretend you are on a **f**lying carpet.
- Make **f**oil sculptures.
- Create a **F**lat Stanley Project.
- **F**ly kids on **f**eet.
- Set off or go watch **f**ireworks (make sure it is legal in your state; use sparklers—with parental supervision).
- Make **f**udge.
- Make up a **f**airy tale or tell one.
- Send a **f**ax to your **f**ather.
- Have a **f**east.
- Watch **f**ireworks.
- Try different **f**lavors at an ice-cream store.
- Wear **f**lip-**f**lops.
- Play **f**risbee.
- Throw a **f**ootball.
- Make your **f**ingerprints using an ink pad.
- Send **f**an mail to someone who is **f**amous (that your child admires).
- Teach the best way to **f**all.
- Make cookies or brownies and take them to your local **f**ire department.
- Make today a **F**amily Day.
- Build **f**orts out of blankets over chairs, beds, and tables. Use a box **f**an to blow into tent.

Math Ideas:
- **F**ractions: Introduce by slicing pies, cookies, sandwiches or a paper pie into 1/2, 1/4, 1/3, etc.
- Explain **F**ahrenheit on a thermometer.

Science Ideas:
- Learn about **f**alcons, **f**ire ants, **f**lamingos, and **f**ish.
- Learn about the life cycle of a **f**rog.
- Discuss what happens in the **f**all.

• Make your own fossils: Fill up containers with dirt (like clay, not potting soil) and water to the consistency of mud. Stir in objects such as shells, wood, leaves rocks, even small toys. Pour on waxed paper and wait to dry. Carefully break open and observe imprints of objects. Most fossils take years to make (from *More Mudpies to Magnets*, 87).
• Study the history of flight with Orville and Wilbur Wright.
• Change the colors of flowers. Buy white carnations, cut off about 1/2 an inch from the bottom, and put in different vases with different colors of food coloring and water mixed. It will change the color of the petals.

Social Studies Ideas:
• Flags: Color free on-line printable state and country flags.
• Color a printable flag of the United States.
• Discover what Henry Ford did for transportation in our country.
• Family: Draw and describe different roles within your family and how you support each other.
• Understand the definition of freedom.
• Learn about France.
• Learn a dozen or more words, a song, and how to say hello and goodbye in French.
• Visit a French restaurant or try some French recipes.

Vocations: Farmer, FBI agent, financial analyst, fireman, fisherman, fitness trainer, flight attendant, florist, football player

Books:
• Fairy tales
• *Five True Dog Stories* by Margaret Davidson
• *The Rainbow Fish* by Marcus Pfister
• *Ferdinand* by Munro Leaf
• *The Foot Book* by Dr. Seuss
• *The Story of Ferdinand* by Munro Leaf
• *Follow the Drinking Gourd* by Jeanette Winter
• *Five Little Monkeys Jumping on the Bed* by Eileen Christelow
• *Frog and Toad Are Friends* by Arnold Lobel
• *Flat Stanley* by Jeff Brown

Music Appreciation:
Folk music, fandango, flamenco, songs of the fifties , fiddle playing, flute playing. Listen to folk songs.

Composers:
Gabriel Fauré 1845–1924, César Franck 1822–1890, Frederic Chopin 1810–1849

 Hymn: "Faith of Our Fathers"

 **Songs:** "The Farmer in the Dell," "Fiddle-de-dee," "Father Abraham," "Frog Went a Courtin' "

 Movies to Watch: *Fantasia, Finding Nemo, Fly Away Home* (PG), *The Fox and The Hound, Frosty The Snowman, Frozen*

Notes:

_____

_____

_____

_____

_____

_____

_____

_____

The Letter G

  Sound : /g/, /j/ (goose, gym)

 Kinesthetic: Form letters out of play-dough, your body, or make letters outside from nature (sticks, leaves, petals, pinecones, etc.).

 Alphabet Notebook
- **Block Letter Pages:** Glue glitter onto your block letter G's page.

- **Clip Art Pages:** Cut and paste clip art onto your G's page.

 **Handwriting Pages:** Practice several upper and lower case letters every day this week.

Menu Ideas: Gala apples, garbanzo beans (chickpeas), garlic, garlic bread, gazpacho, German chocolate cake, German potato salad, German sausage, ginger ale, gingerbread, ginger snaps, gnocchi, Godiva™ chocolate, Goldfish Crackers™, Good and Plenty™ candy, Gouda cheese, graham crackers, granola, grapes, grape juice, grapefruit, grapefruit juice, Greek yogurt, green beans, green jello, green olives, green onions, green peppers, grits, guacamole, gum, gummy bears, gyros

 Field Trip Ideas: Watch a glass blower. Go to a goat farm or a granite countertop store. Go to a Greek festival. Visit a greenhouse or a grocery store tour.

Bible Ideas:
Gabriel, Gad, Gideon, God, Goliath and David, The Good Samaritan, and teach the Good News of the Gospel
- **Missionaries:** George Muller (1805–1898), England. Be sure to tell the story about the children in the orphanage waiting at an empty table for breakfast; Gladys Aylward (1902–1970), China

Copy Work & Memory Verse: "...God is love" (I John 4:8).

Character Traits: Generous, **g**iving, **g**entle, **g**rateful, **g**racious

Art:
- Make a **G**od's eye with popsicles sticks and yarn.
- **G**litter and **g**lue art: Using **g**lue, design a picture by squeezing it out of bottle. Then add **g**litter.
- Draw a **g**iant.
- **G**lue something.

Artist Study: Vincent Van **G**ogh. I recommend the book, *Camille and The Sunflowers* by Laurence Anholt

Poetry:
Mother Goose:
GEORGY PORGY
Georgy Porgy, pudding and pie,
Kissed the girls and made them cry.
When the boys came out to play,
Georgy Porgy ran away.

Activities:
- **G**iggle.
- Look up the world's tallest man (**g**iant).
- Visit, call, or write **g**randma and **g**randpa.
- Make a **g**ratitude journal.
- **G**o get **g**as.
- **G**o to the **g**rocery store.
- Learn the **G**olden Rule.
- Make a **g**lass band: Using different shaped **g**lass containers, fill with various levels of water, and ting each with a spoon around the rim. Each container will make a different sound.
- Chew **g**um.
- Practice **g**roaning; kids love this.
- **G**rate **g**arlic and cook in a pan; taste it and use the rest for dinner.
- Buy a **g**um ball out of a **g**um ball machine.
- Try **g**oat's milk.
- Take dog to a **g**roomer or **g**room it yourself; have child help in small ways.
- Have fun in the bath, at the movies, and in balloons with **g**low sticks.
- Play **g**ames with **g**low sticks such as tag and hide-and-seek.
- **G**ive something away.
- Discuss the dangers of **g**uns.

- Make up a **g**ame.
- Play a board **g**ame such as Candy-land™, Chutes and Ladders™, Hi Ho Cheerio™; have an official **g**ame day. Invite friends to play.
- Collect **g**arbage from around your house and take out the **g**arbage with your child. Better yet, take child to the dump see what happens to **g**arbage.
- Do something nice for your **g**arbage men.
- Have a **g**arage sale.
- **G**rate cheese or carrots.
- Make a **g**ingerbread house.
- Play **g**olf or mini **g**olf. Hit a **g**olf ball.
- Do some **g**ymnastics (cartwheels, somersault, handstand).
- Demonstrate **g**reediness and compare to **g**ratefulness.
- Clean your **g**arage with your child. Play music and make it fun.

 Math Ideas:
- Introduce the **g**reater than symbol ($>$).
- Sort like items in **g**roups—buttons, play food, rocks, etc.
- Play with a **g**eo board. Make your own **g**eo board.
- **G**rams: Using a **g**ram scale, measure food items.

 Science Ideas:
- Learn about **g**orillas, **g**eese, **g**iraffes, **g**laciers, **g**ravity, or **g**ears.
- Make a miniature **g**arden with foil pie pans, moss, sand, stones, gemstones, and twigs for trees.
- **G**ardening: Plant bulbs or seeds.
- **G**row **g**rass in a cup.

 Social Studies Ideas:
- Introduce a **g**lobe; locate where you live.
- Learn about **G**reece, **G**ermany, **g**ypsies, or the **G**reat Wall of China.
- Learn a dozen or more words, a song, and how to say hello and goodbye in **G**erman.
- **G**o to a **G**reek restaurant; try a **g**yro (pronounced *hero*).
- Visit a **G**erman restaurant or try some **G**erman recipes.

 Vocations: **G**arbage collector, **g**ardener, **g**eologist, **g**enealogist, **g**lass maker blower, **g**raphic designer, **g**reeting card writer, **g**rocery store manager, **g**roomer, **g**uard, **g**ymnast

Books:
- *A Grain of Rice* by Helena Clare Pittman
- *In Grandma's Attic* by Arleta Richardson
- *The Golden Goose* retold by Uri Shulevitz
- *The Three Billy Goats Gruff* by Paul Galdone
- *Goodnight Moon* by Margaret Wise Brown
- *The Big Green Pocketbook* by Candice Ransom
- *The Glorious Flight* by Alice and Martin Provensen
- *Mr. Gumpy's Motor Car* by John Burningham
- *The Giraffe That Walked to Paris* by Nancy Milton
- *The Giving Tree* by Shel Silverstein

Music Appreciation:
Gospel music, guitar solos

Composers:
George Gershwin 1898–1937, Edvard Grieg 1843–1907

Hymn: "Great Is Thy Faithfulness" or "Go Tell It on the Mountain"

Songs: "The Green Grass Grew All Around" and "Amazing Grace"

Movies to Watch: *The Great Mouse Detective, G-Force, Gulliver's Travels*

The Letter H

 Sound : /h/ (horse)

 Kinesthetic: Form letters out of play-dough, your body, or make letters outside from nature (sticks, leaves, petals, pinecones, etc.).

 Alphabet Notebook
• **Block Letter Pages:** Glue **h**air or **h**earts onto your block letter **H**'s page. Make **h**oles (with a **h**ole punch) and glue on to the letter **H**.

• **Clip Art Pages:** Cut and paste clip art onto your **H**'s page.

Handwriting Pages: Practice several upper and lower case letters every day this week.

 Menu Ideas: Haddock, **h**alf and **h**alf, **h**alibut, **h**am, **h**am and cheese roll-ups, **h**am and cheese croissants, **h**am and cheese grilled sandwiches, **h**amburger, **h**ash browns, **h**azelnuts, **h**azelnut spread, **h**eart shaped cookies, **h**earts of palm, **H**ershey Chocolate™ bar, **H**ershey's Kisses™, **h**oagie, **h**ominy, **h**oney, **h**oney buns, **h**oney dew, **h**oney graham crackers, **h**oney and tea, **h**oney and toast, **h**orse radish (just taste), **h**ot cocoa, **h**ot dogs, **H**ot Pockets™, **h**ot wings, **h**ummus

 Field Trip Ideas: Meet someone who is **h**andicapped. Go to a **h**ardware store; climb in a **h**elicopter; go **h**iking; watch a **h**istorical re-enactment; walk on a **h**istorical trail; enjoy **h**orseback riding (or go and visit a **h**orse); go to a **h**otel or **h**ospital.

 Bible Ideas:
Habakkuk, **H**aggai, **H**aman, **H**annah, **H**eaven, **H**ebrews, **H**ezekiah, the **H**oly Spirit, **H**osea, **H**ur

• **Missionary:** **H**udson Taylor (1832–1905), China

Copy Work & Memory Verse: "Honor thy father and thy mother..." (Exodus 20:12).

Character Traits: Happy, hard-working, helpful, honest, hopeful, humble, humorous

Art:
• Make handiwork a part of your every day. It is okay if the project carries over into another week.
• Create a handprint poem.
• Discover handprint art—angel wings, butterflies, reindeer, trees, wreaths, and more (http://rainbowswithinreach.blogspot.com/2012/08 handprint-poems-projects.html).
• Make a heart wreath by gluing cut-out hearts on the rim of a paper plate. Cut a hole in the center of the plate.
• Trace your hands.
• Teach child to draw a heart (M on top; V on bottom).

Artist Study: Winslow Homer, American Painter

Poetry:
Haiku
A haiku must have 17 syllables. The format of a haiku is often described as 5-7-5.
• The first line has five syllables. The second line has seven syllables. The third line has five syllables.
• Explain a syllable, a one-unit sound. Attempt a "What Am I?" haiku that is written as a riddle.
• Read some haikus by poets and haikus written by children.

Mother Goose:
HUMPTY DUMPTY
Humpty Dumpty sat on a wall,
Humpty Dumpty had a great fall;
All the King's horses, and all the King's men
Cannot put Humpty Dumpty together again.

Activities:
• Play horseshoes.
• Play water fun with the hose.
• Learn how to hula-hoop.
• Taste honey.
• Sing and dance the "Hokey Pokey."
• Ride a horse, or see if you can feed an apple or a carrot to a horse.
• Buy a new hairbrush.

- Teach child how to **h**ammer a nail in a block of wood (parental supervision required).
- Practice **h**ugging.
- Measure your child's **h**eight.
- Make funny **h**air-dos with your child (I double dog dare you to wear yours out!).
- Teach child how to give a firm **h**andshake that is neither too hard nor too soft.
- Try on **h**ats.
- Make a newspaper **h**at.
- Play "**h**orsey" with child on your knee.
- Play **h**angman.
- **H**ost a party.
- **H**op on one leg then two.
- Practice **h**and shadows. It is amazing what **h**ands can do.
- Learn how to play **h**opscotch.
- Visit a **h**en.
- Watch a **h**orse race.
- Relax in a **h**ammock.
- Go **h**iking.
- Stay at a **h**otel.
- Show child a **h**undred dollar bill.
- Find someone to **h**elp.
- Play **h**ide-n-seek together. Try playing in the dark with a flashlight.
- Play **h**ot potato.
- Get a **h**aircut.

Math Ideas:
- Count by 100s (**h**undreds).
- Show **h**ours (o'clocks) on a clock.
- Show **h**emispheres on a globe.
- Measure your child's **h**eight today and at the end of the year see how much she/he has grown.
- Draw a **h**exagon.
- Demonstrate **h**orizontal.
- Time something with an **h**ourglass.
- Learn about **h**olograms.

Science Ideas:
- Learn about the **h**ippopotamuses, **h**umpback whales, **h**orses, and **h**urricanes.
- Study **h**elicopters.
- Teach the meaning of an **h**erbivore.
- Watch a **h**ammerhead shark.
- Learn about **h**oming pigeons.
- Learn about the **h**uman **h**eart.

Social Studies Ideas:
- Hawaii
- Print child's name in hieroglyphics.
- Discuss habitats.
- Discuss human rights.
- Learn about the homeless in your area. Create blessing bags to give them.

Vocations: Harpist, helicopter pilot, historian, home health nurse, horticulturalist

Books:
- *Horton Hatches an Egg* by Dr. Suess
- *Harry the Dirty Dog* by Gene Zion
- *My Hands* by Aliki
- *The Hundred Dresses* by Eleanor Estes
- *Old Hat New Hat* by Stan and Jan Berenstain
- *How To Make an Apple Pie and See the World* by Marjorie Priceman
- *Harold and the Purple Crayon* by Crockett Johnson

Music Appreciation:
Hymns, holiday music, harpist; hillbilly music, hip hop music.
Watch a handbell performance.

Composers:
George Frideric Handel 1685–1759. Watch Handel's Messiah (in person if you can).
Franz Joseph Haydn 1736–1809

Hymn: "How Great Thou Art"

Songs: "If You're Happy and You Know It," "Home on the Range," "The Hokey Pokey," "He's Got the Whole World in His Hands"

Movies to Watch: *Happy Feet, Harriet The Spy, Heidi, Herbie, Hercules, Home Alone* (PG), *Honey, I Shrunk the Kids, How to Train Your Dragon (1 & 2), The Hunchback of Notre Dame, Adventures of Huck Finn*

Notes:

The Letter I

 Sound : /i/, /I/ (it, ivy)

 Kinesthetic: Form letters out of play-dough, your body, or make letters outside from nature (sticks, leaves, petals, pinecones, etc.).

 Alphabet Notebook
• **Block Letter Pages:** Draw or glue aluminum icicles (thin, upside down triangles) hanging off your **Is**. Draw inchworms on your block letter **I**'s page.

• **Clip Art Pages:** Cut and paste clip art onto your **I**'s page.

Ii **Handwriting Pages:** Practice several upper and lower case letters every day this week.

 Menu Ideas: ice (make colored ice cubes with food coloring), iceberg lettuce, ice tea, icing, ice-cream, ice-cream sandwich, Icee™, Icicle Pops™, Irish coffee, an "iron sandwich" (put bread and cheese between waxed paper and iron), Italian bread, Italian ice, Italian salad dressing

 Field Trip Ideas: Ice cream factory. Go ice-skating; visit an iguana at a pet store; or go to an Indian museum or Indian reservation. Take child to nursery at church to see infants.

 Bible Ideas:
Ichabod, idols, Isaac, Isaiah, Issachar, Ishmael, Israel

• **Missionary:** Ida Scudder (1870–1960), India

Copy Work & Memory Verse: "If ye shall ask any thing in My name, I will do it" (John 14:14).

Character Traits: Independent, imaginative, inquisitive, inventive

Art:
- Make an Indian headband with cardboard, feathers, and paint.
- Draw and color an inchworm.
- Make icicles: Glue upside down triangles made out of aluminum foil (long and skinny) from branches on brown paper.
- Draw insects.
- Use an ink pad and stamp.

Poetry:

Mother Goose:
IF ALL THE SEAS WERE ONE SEA
If all the seas were one sea,
What a *great* sea that would be!
And if all the trees were one tree,
What a *great* tree that would be!
And if all the axes were one axe,
What a *great* axe that would be!
And if all the men were one man,
What a *great* man he would be!
And if the *great* man took the *great* axe,
And cut down the *great* tree,
And let it fall into the *great* sea,
What a splish splash *that* would be!

Activities:
- Play an instrument(s).
- Make homemade ice-cream in a sealable plastic bag.
- Burn incense (parental supervision required).
- Draw a picture with ink (you can make a quill with a feather).
- Dress up and pretend to be an Indian. Paint child's face too.
- Catch or buy insects. "Children should be encouraged to watch, patiently and quietly, until they learn something of the habits and history of bee, ant, wasp, spider, hairy caterpillar, dragon-fly, and whatever of larger growth comes in their way." ~ Charlotte Mason (Vol 1, II, *Out-Of-Door Life For The Children*, 57).
- Make colored ice cubes using food coloring and enjoy in a refreshing drink.
- Make your own ice-cream sandwiches with cookies; ice-cream in the middle, wrap and place in freezer.
- Play the imitation game. Have the "followers" imitate the leader. Take turns being the leader around your home or yard.
- Draw a picture with different colored ink pens.
- Ice icing on a cake with your child. Remember it doesn't have to be perfect. It will still taste good regardless. Let your child do it!

- Use your imagination and make up a story or game.
- Show your child pictures of him/herself when he/she was an infant.
- Discuss injury and infections.
- Scratch an itch.
- Plant ivy or notice it growing while out.
- Interview your child—favorite color, subject, friend, food, etc.
- Interview an elderly relative (grandparent) or neighbor about their "favorites" and their past.

Math Ideas:
- Inches: Measure things in your house or yard with a ruler or tape measure in inches.
- Teach the idea of infinite. Quote Buzz Light Year, "To infinity and beyond."
- Intersection: Show how streets and lines intersect.
- Teach integers.
- Draw an isosceles triangle.

Science Ideas:
- Learn about iguanas.
- Insects—collect insects; make an insect shadow box this year.
- Learn the 3 parts of an insect.
- Make your own invisible ink. (http://www.amazing-preschool-activities.com/preschool-science-invisible-ink.html)

Social Studies Ideas:
- Learn about American Indians and their different tribes.
- Visit an Indian restaurant and try something new.
- Try an Italian restaurant.
- Learn about Iran, Iraq, and Italy (show how Italy is shaped like a boot).
- Discover American inventors.
- Discuss income taxes—taxes paid by households and businesses on the income they receive.

Vocations: Illustrator, importer, insurance agent, interior designer, interpreter

Books:
- *Ian and the Giant Leafy Obstacle* by Shelia Miller
- *If You Give a Mouse a Cookie* by Laura Numeroff

- *Inch by Inch* by Leo Lionni
- *The Igloo* by Charlotte and David Yue
- *If You Lived with the Sioux Indians* by Ann McGovern
- *I Am an Artist* by Pat L. Collins

 Music Appreciation:
Instrumental music, Indian music (traditional Native American and India),
Indian flute music with R. Carlos Nakai (he is really amazing), Irish folk, Irish step-dancing

 Composers:
Charles Ives 1874–1954

 Hymn: "It Is Well"

 Songs: "Ten Little Indians," "The Itsy Bitsy Spider"

 Movies to Watch: *Adventures of Ichabod and Mr. Toad, The Incredible Journey, The Incredibles, Inside Out, Into the Woods*

Notes:

_____

_____

_____

_____

_____

_____

_____

The Letter J

 Sound : /j/ (jam)

 Kinesthetic: Form letters out of play-dough, your body, or make letters outside from nature (sticks, leaves, petals, pinecones, etc.).

 Alphabet Notebook
• **Block Letter Pages:** Glue craft jewels onto your Js or draw multi-colored jelly beans on your block letter J's page.

• **Clip Art Pages:** Cut and paste clip art onto your J's page.

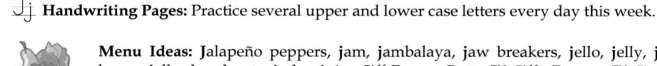 **Handwriting Pages:** Practice several upper and lower case letters every day this week.

 Menu Ideas: Jalapeño peppers, jam, jambalaya, jaw breakers, jello, jelly, jelly beans, jelly doughnuts, jerky, juice, Jiff Peanut Butter™, Jiffy Popcorn™, Jimmy Dean Sausage™, johnny cake, Jolly Rancher™ candy, juice, Juicy Fruit™ gum, juice pops, Ju-Ju Fruit™ candy, junk food

 Field Trip Ideas: Visit a jail, jeweler, a journalist. Enjoy a jungle gym at a park with jam sandwiches. Take trash to a junkyard.

 Bible Ideas:
Jesus: His birth, His parables; John the Baptist, Jonah, Joseph and the coat of many colors, Jacob, James, Jeremiah, Jerusalem, Jews, Job, Joel, John 3:16, Joshua, Joseph, Judah, Jude, Judges

• **Missionaries:** John Wesley (1703–1791), England; Jonathan Edwards (1703–1758), America; Jim Elliot (1927–1956), Ecuador

Copy Work & Memory Verse: "Jesus saith unto him, I am the way, the truth, and the life: no man cometh unto the Father, but by Me" (John 14:6).
Character Traits: Jovial, joyful

 Art:
• Make jewelry with beads, macaroni, rhinestones, etc., and dental floss for string.
• Make jewelry with painted or colored dyed pasta and string yarn.
• Make Joseph's coat of many colors with colored tissue.

 Poetry:

Mother Goose:
JACK AND JILL
  Jack and Jill went up the hill,
 To fetch a pail of water;
Jack fell down, and broke his crown,
 And Jill came tumbling after.

Then up Jack got and off did trot,
 As fast as he could caper,
To old Dame Dob, who patched his nob
 With vinegar and brown paper.

 Activities:
• Attempt to juggle (start with 2 balls; then add a third).
• Play with jumprope, single or double Dutch.
• See how many jumping jacks you can do.
• Buy jumping beans.
• Play with a jack-in-the-box.
• Carve a jack-o'-lantern (real or paper).
• Learn a joke and tell someone.
• Finish a jigsaw puzzle.
• Make beef jerky with a dehydrator or oven.
• Wear jeans.
• Go on a journey.
• Jar penny drop: Put a shot glass or small glass into a large pickle jar (ask a deli restaurant for one free) and drop pennies in from top. Try to get pennies into the little glass in the jar.
• Play jacks.
• Jump.

- See who can jump the farthest; use masking tape.
- Dress up with jewelry.
- Ride in a jeep.
- Discuss jealousy.
- Watch the jitterbug dance.
- Watch the jive dance.
- Learn "Jesus Loves Me" in sign language.

Math Ideas:
- Count with jelly beans.
- Count jumping jacks.

Science Ideas:
- Learn about jaguar and jellyfish.
- Investigate how jet engines and jet airplanes work.
- Discover facts about Jupiter and observe online or through a telescope.

Social Studies Ideas:
- Learn about Japan, Jerusalem, or Jamaica, and find on map or globe.
- Eat at a Japanese restaurant.
- Listen to the Japanese language on-line. Learn several words.
- Read about John F. Kennedy, Thomas Jefferson, or Joan of Arc.

Vocations: Janitor, jazz musician, jailor, jeweler, jewelry designer, journalist, journeyman, judge

Books:
- *Jack and The Bean Stalk* English Folktale
- *Johnny Appleseed: The Story of a Legend*
- *Jesse Bear, What Will You Wear?* by NW Carlstrom
- *The Giant Jam Sandwich* by John Vernon Lord
- *If Jesus Came to My House* by Joan Gale Thomas
- *Jelly Beans for Sale* by Bruce McMillan

Music Appreciation:
Japanese pop, jazz

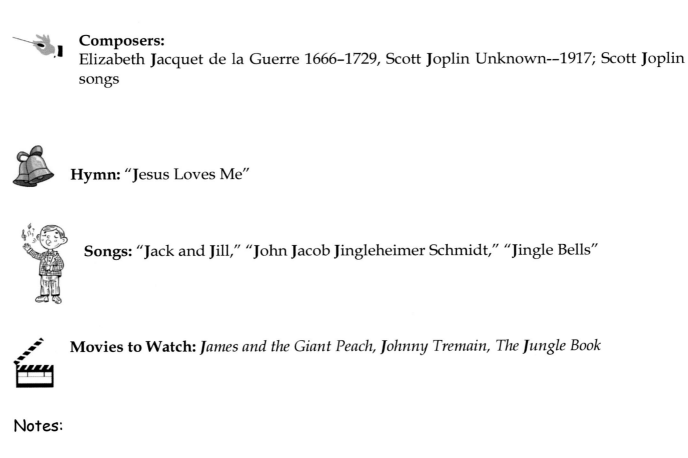

Composers:
Elizabeth Jacquet de la Guerre 1666–1729, Scott Joplin Unknown--1917; Scott Joplin songs

Hymn: "Jesus Loves Me"

Songs: "Jack and Jill," "John Jacob Jingleheimer Schmidt," "Jingle Bells"

Movies to Watch: *James and the Giant Peach, Johnny Tremain, The Jungle Book*

Notes:

_____

_____

_____

_____

_____

_____

_____

_____

_____

The Letter K

 Sound : /k/ (kite)

 Kinesthetic: Form letters out of play-dough, your body, or make letters outside from nature (sticks, leaves, petals, pinecones, etc.).

 Alphabet Notebook
• **Block Letter Pages:** Kiss your Ks with lipstick or make a crayon rubbing of keys or glue Kool-aid™ onto your block letter K's page.

• **Clip Art Pages:** Cut and paste clip art onto your K's page.

Kk **Handwriting Pages:** Practice several upper and lower case letters every day this week.

 Menu Ideas: Kabobs (grilled chicken and beef or cubed ham and cheese and grape tomatoes and cucumbers on a kabob), kaiser roll, kale (green leafy vegetable), kale chips, KFC™ chicken, Keebler™ cookies, kefir, Kellogg's Special K™ cereal, key lime pie, kidney beans, kielbasa, kimchee (Korean fermented cabbage relish), ketchup, kettle corn, Hershey's Kisses™, kite cookies, Kit-Kat™ bar, kiwi, Kix™ cereal, Klondike™ bars, Kool-Aide™, Kraft™ cheese, kumquats

 Field Trip Ideas: Go to a kid's museum, kitchen of a big restaurant (just ask!), or K-Mart™. Do a Krispy Kreme™ tour.

 Bible Ideas:
King Solomon, Jesus' kindness, Kings of the Bible, Kish, Korah,

• **Missionary:** Klaus-Dieter John (1960), Peru

Copy Work & Memory Verse: "Keep thy tongue from evil..." (Psalm 34:13).

Character Traits: Kindness

Art:
• Make a kaleidoscope with a Pringles™ can or make a kaleidoscope with a paper towel tube and plastic report cover.
• For girls: Kiss a piece of paper (with lipstick) and send to a family member in the mail.
• For boys: Have child kiss a letter, take a picture of child kissing letter, and mail to family member in the mail.
• Draw koalas and kangaroos. Find easy instructions online.
• Learn how to knit with your child.

Poetry:
Read some of Rudyard Kipling's Poems
"Rikki-Tikki-Tavi" by Rudyard Kipling

Mother Goose:
THE KILKENNY CATS
There were once two cats of Kilkenny.
Each thought there was one cat too many;
So they fought and they fit,
And they scratched and they bit,
Till, excepting their nails,
And the tips of their tails,
Instead of two cats, there weren't any.

Activities:
• Go to hobby store and look through kaleidoscopes.
• Buy a kaleidoscope and start a collection (we love ours; you are never too old!).
• Learn to tie knots with rope or thread for sewing (get book from the library).
• Perform a *random act of kindness* known AND anonymous to a stranger and a neighbor. Google for ideas of ARK (acts of random kindness). Count these and attempt to reach 1,000,000 random acts of kindness!
• Make a letter **K** with your body.
• Play kickball.
• Kick a ball.
• Play a kazoo.

- Fly a **k**ite.
- Use a **K**leenex™.
- Heat water in a **k**ettle and hear it whistle.
- Peruse Little **K**eepers at Home curriculum for ideas.
- Make or learn about **k**imonos,
- Clean the **k**itchen.
- Talk about **k**indergarten.
- Pet a **k**itten.
- **K**iss your mom, dad, or someone you love.
- **K**nead dough.
- Watch **k**ung fu kicks.
- Read from a **K**ing James Bible.
- Allow child to type their name on a **k**eyboard.
- Make crayon or pencil rubbings with a **k**ey.
- Trace a **k**ey.
- Take child to hardware store and watch a **k**ey being copied and cut.

 Math Ideas:
- Introduce **k**ilo — kilograms, kilometers. kiloliters.
- Walk a **k**ilometer.

 Science Ideas:
- Learn about **k**angaroos, koala bears, or komodo dragons.
- Make a **k**ite. Fly it!
- Learn about Benjamin Franklin and his **k**ite experiment.

 Social Studies Ideas:
- Learn about famous **k**ings in history.
- People who made important contributions to the world: Helen **K**eller, Martin Luther **K**ing, Jr., etc.
- Study **K**ing Arthur and the **K**nights of the Round Table.
- Learn about **K**orea.
- Visit a **K**orean restaurant and try some **k**imchi.

 Vocations: **K**arate instructor, key maker, kindergarten teacher

 Books:
- *The Korean Cinderella* by Shirley Climo
- *The Emperor and the Kite* by Jane Yolen

- *Three Little Kittens* Nursery Rhyme
- *A Kiss for Little Bear* by Else Holmelund Minarik
- *Katy No-Pocket* by Emmy Payne
- *Katy and the Big Snow* by Virginia Lee Burton
- *Mrs. Katz and Tush* by Patricia Polacco

Music Appreciation:
Perform **k**araoke. Use a **k**araoke machine and microphone, or pretend to sing into a hairbrush.

Composers:
Dmitri **K**abalevsky 1904–1987, Zoltán **K**odály 1882–1967

Hymn: Sing "**K**um Ba Ya" and discover the story behind it.

Songs: "**K**ookaburra," "The Three Little **K**ittens"

Movies to Watch: *The Karate Kid*, *Kidnapped* (PG), *Kung Fu Panda*

Notes:

_____

_____

_____

_____

_____

_____

The Letter L

 Sound : /l/ (lion)

 Kinesthetic: Form letters out of play-dough, your body, or make letters outside from nature (sticks, leaves, petals, pinecones, etc.).

 Alphabet Notebook
• **Block Letter Pages:** Glue leaves onto your block letter L's page and then press to flatten; make leaf rubbings or glue lace (from paper doilies) on your Ls; or make lines inside the **L** letters.

• **Clip Art Pages:** Cut and paste clip art onto your L's page.

Handwriting Pages: Practice several upper and lower case letters every day this week.

 Menu Ideas: Ladyfingers, lamb, lasagna, latte, leeks, lemon bars, lemon cake, lemon cookies (sugar cookies with a few drops of lemon), lemon ice-cubes (add to water for a refreshing drink), homemade lemonade, lemons, lemon meringue pie, lemon poppy seed muffins, lentils, lettuce (all types), licorice, Life™ cereal, Life Savers™, lima beans, limes, linguini, liver, lobster, lollipop, London broil, Luigi's™ (lemon)

 Field Trip Ideas: Meet a lawyer. Go to the library. Climb a lighthouse. Visit a llama farm. Speak to a locksmith. Go to a lumberyard.

 Bible Ideas:
The Last Supper, the leper who was healed, the Lord's Prayer, Parable of the Lost Coin, Love verses in the Bible (1 Corinthians 13), Laban, Lazarus, Levi, the Lord, Lot, Luke, Lydia

• **Missionary:** Lottie Moon (1840–1912), China

Copy Work & Memory Verse: "Look unto Me, and be ye saved..." (Isaiah 45:22).

Character Traits: Leader, likable, loving, loyal

 Art:
- Paint lace doilies on canvas or paper using cloth or paper doilies.
- Draw a ladybug or a lion on a paper plate.
- Learn latch hooking with a latch hook kit.
- Make a lap book on letters, love, or leaves.
- Make a lanyard.
- Make leaf rubbings: Place leaves under a piece of white paper, and color with the side of the crayon lightly until the leaf print and veins come through to the paper.
- Use leaf identification to identify types of trees.
- Make leaf prints by dipping leaves in paint.
- Collect vibrant leaves and press between 2 pieces of clear contact paper to make a placemat.
- Use a light box to trace leaves or pictures.

Artist Study: Leonardo da Vinci, The Last Supper

 Poetry:
Limericks: Read some, make one up, and laugh!
There was an Old Man with a beard,
Who said, "It is just as I feared!
Two Owls and a Hen,
Four Larks and a Wren,
Have all built their nests in my beard!"
By Edward Lear

- Read some of Henry Wadsworth Longfellow's poems.
- *Poetry for Young People: Henry Wadsworth Longfellow* by Henry Wadsworth Longfellow
- "Hiawatha" by Henry Wadsworth Longfellow
- "Paul Revere's Ride" by Henry Wadsworth Longfellow

Mother Goose:
LITTLE BOY BLUE
Little Boy Blue, come, blow your horn!
The sheep's in the meadow, the cow's in the corn.
Where's the little boy that looks after the sheep?
Under the haystack, fast asleep!

Activities:
- Write a letter.
- Create a lollipop tree (paint styrofoam cone and stick lollipops in it like a tree).
- Make lavender sachets with tulle, lavender, and ribbon.
- Make lacing cards with paper plates or craft foam.
- Play limbo.
- Learn about love.
- Rake leaves into a pile and jump!
- Pretend to lose something or when you do lose something, point it out to your child and pray that God will help you find it.
- Play leap frog.
- Laugh! Listen to others laughing if you need help. Try the ultimate laugh challenge.
- Count how many times you laugh in a day.
- Smell lavender and lemongrass essential oils.
- Use lotion.
- Go to the library.
- Build something with Legos™.
- Make your own homemade laundry detergent with your child.
- Teach child how to wash a load of laundry.
- Let child wallow in a fresh load of warm laundry.
- Teach child to listen, really listen. Have child close eyes (or blindfold) while you make sounds (knock, whisper, bang on different objects, like glass, metal, wood, paper). Have child guess what made the sound.
- Play Lincoln Logs™.
- Play with linking cubes by color or pattern.
- Change a lightbulb.
- Cuddle child on your lap.
- Lend your child something.
- Be lazy for a couple hours.
- Play follow-the-leader: Follow child around your house or yard, and mimic everything she/he says and go everywhere she/he goes.
- Go to a nearby lake to swim or picnic.
- Lick a lollipop.
- Be loud outside.
- Put child's lunch in a lunchbox this week.
- Play the license plate game in the car, or just look for the letter of the week on license plates.
- Try to catch leaves when they are falling from the trees. Offer prize to the winner for the most leaves caught.

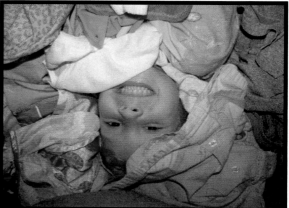

Math Ideas:
• Draw lines—line segments, crooked, straight, zig-zag, parallel, horizontal, and vertical.
• Explain a leap year.
• Explain less than (<).

Science Ideas:
• Learn about lions, lobsters, leopards, or lizards.
• Discover light; ROYGBIV (red, orange, yellow, green, blue, indigo, violet)
• Make your own lever.
• Buy a lady bug house kit.
• Find lichen in your yard.
• Find the Little Dipper in the constellations.

Social Studies Ideas:
• Abraham Lincoln, Robert E. Lee, Meriwether Lewis
• Learn about the Statue of Liberty.
• Learn about Sir Lancelot.

Vocations: Landscape artist, lawyer, librarian, life guard, locksmith

Books:
• *Lentil* by Robert McCloskey
• *The Grouchy Ladybug* by Eric Carle
• *Tawny Scrawny Lion* by Kathryn Jackson
• *The Little Red Lighthouse and the Great Gray Bridge* by Hildegarde H. Swift
• *Ladybug, Ladybug* by Ruth Brown
• *The Little Rabbit* by Judy Dunn

Music Appreciation:
Latin music, lullabies

Composers:
Libby Larsen 1950, Franz Liszt 1811–1886

Hymn: "Leaning on the Everlasting Arms," "Lord of the Dance" (Celtic Hymn)

 Songs: "On the Good Ship Lollipop," "I Love You" (from Barney), "London Bridge"

 Movies to Watch: *Lady and the Tramp, The Lego Movie, Lilo and Stitch, Lion King, Little House on the Prairie, The Little Mermaid, The Little Princess, The Lorax, I Love Lucy*

Notes:

_____

_____

_____

_____

_____

_____

_____

_____

_____

_____

The Letter M

 Sound : /m/ (mom)

 Kinesthetic: Form letters out of play-dough, your body, or make letters outside from nature (sticks, leaves, petals, pinecones, etc.).

 Alphabet Notebook
- **Block Letter Pages:** Cut up an old **m**ap or **m**agazine pictures and glue onto your block letter **M**'s page. Or color **M**'s with **m**arkers.

- **Clip Art Pages:** Cut and paste clip art onto your **M**'s page.

Handwriting Pages: Practice several upper and lower case letters every day this week.

 Menu Ideas: **M**acadamia nuts, **m**acaroni and cheese, **m**acaroon cookies, **m**andarin oranges, **m**angoes, **m**anicotti, **M**ars™ bars, **m**arshmallows (small and large), **m**armalade, **m**aple syrup, **m**ashed potatoes, **m**atzo balls, **m**ayonnaise, **m**elons, **m**eatballs, **m**eatloaf, **m**elba toast, **m**elons, **M**ilano cookies, **M**ilky Way™ candy bars, **M**ike and Ike's™ candy, **m**ilk, **m**ilk shakes, **m**int ice-cream, **m**onkey bread, **M**oon Pies™, **m**ousse, **m**ozzarella cheese, **m**uesli, **m**uffins, **m**ushrooms (sautéed or stuffed)

 Field Trip Ideas: Play **m**iniature golf or go to a **m**ovie theater. Do some **m**usic appreciation (symphony or concert). **M**eet a **m**usician. Go to a **m**anufacturing plant.

 Bible Ideas:
Magi, **M**artha and **M**ary, **M**ary (Jesus' mother), **M**atthew, **M**elchizadek, **M**ephibosheth, **M**icah, **M**ichael, **m**iracles, **M**iriam, **M**ordecai, **M**oses

- **Missionary:** **M**ary Slessor (1848–1915), Africa

Copy Work & Memory Verse: "**M**y son, give **M**e thine heart..." (Proverbs 23:26).

Character Traits: Mannerly, **m**ature, **m**eek, **m**erciful, **m**odesty

Art:
- **M**ake a **m**ask from a paper plate, cut out 2 holes for eyes, decorate a face, and use tongue depressors or popsicle sticks for a handle.
- Learn the art of **m**acrame.

- **M**ake a **m**ailbox (or buy one) and use it to write, give, or create special things for your child. Put **m**ailbox in child's room to use when you have a special note or special something. Child can put it in your room when it is their turn to return the favor.

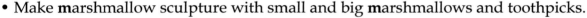

- Create **m**arble art using a **m**arble, paint, and a shoebox. Wet **m**arble in paint and roll in different colors across the paper in the box.
- **M**ake a **m**acaroni necklace. (You can color the **m**acaroni first with food coloring and rubbing alcohol.)
- **M**ake **m**agnets (glue any small lightweight craft to a **m**agnet). Or make **m**arble **m**agnets: Use clear, flat marbles and glue picture to underside, attach magnet, and hang.
- **M**ake **m**osaic **m**urals out of cut-up pieces of construction paper.
- **M**ake **m**edals. Use cardboard wrapped in aluminum or aluminum frozen juice lids. The parent can punch hole with ice pick, string, and hang on neck. (Use for Olympics games on O week.)
- **M**ake **m**arshmallow sculpture with small and big **m**arshmallows and toothpicks.
- **M**ake a **m**ood picture with several faces of **m**oods: happy, sad, angry, surprised.

Artist Study:
- Claude-Oscar **M**onet: I recommend the book, *Katy and The Water Lily Pond* by James Mayhew.
- **M**ichelangelo: Tape paper under kitchen table and have children lie on back to paint upside down like **M**ichelangelo painted the Sistine Chapel. May need to use pillows and washable paint! Child's arms will get tired. Discuss how **M**ichelangelo painted like this for years.

Poetry:
Read some of A.A. **M**ilne's poems

Mother Goose:
MARY, MARY, QUITE CONTRARY
Mary, Mary, quite contrary,
  How does your garden grow?
Silver bells and cockle-shells,
  And pretty maids all of a row.

Activities:
- Discuss **m**aps: Find your country, state, city, town, and street on a **m**ap.
- **M**ake a **m**ap of your home. Help child to draw a **m**ap of the rooms in your home, a **m**ap of your child's room, and where the boundaries of your property are located.
- Let child pay for something with **m**oney.
- Learn **m**anners: Role play situations when you need good **m**anners.
- Discuss the "**m**agic words," *please* and *thank you.*
- Go to a **m**ovie theater.
- Give your child a **m**ake believe **m**ake-over. For girls: blush, lip gloss, and tiara. For boys: a hat and pretend **m**ustache.
- Play a **m**usic box.
- Hang on the **m**onkey bars.
- Buy a **m**agazine or check out children's **m**agazines at your library.
- Discuss your child's best **m**emory.
- Practice **m**arching.
- **M**ake a **m**irror image. **M**irror your child and have your child **m**irror you.
- **M**ail something to someone your child loves. **M**ail your child a letter.
- Do something nice for your **m**ailman.
- **M**end a piece of clothing with your child (button, hem, hole, etc.).
- **M**ake a **m**ess and then clean it.
- Discuss **m**odesty.
- Discuss the **m**eaning of a Godly **m**entor. Help your child to find one.
- **M**ake **m**usic: Oatmeal drum, **M**orocco castanets, **m**usical **m**aracas.
- Play **M**other **M**ay I.
- Play **m**usical chairs.
- **M**ake believe something **m**agical.
- Leave an encouraging **m**essage on the **m**irror with dry erase **m**arkers or when the **m**irror is foggy with your finger.
- Use or **m**ake a **m**old for soap, candy, or popsicles.
- Help child find and glue **m**agazine pictures of all the things your child loves: colors, toys, animals, room decor, etc. onto paper.
- Teach child to use a **m**achine: washing **m**achine, dryer, or **m**ixer (parental supervision required).
- Teach child to **m**op a floor.
- Learn a **m**agic trick. Put on a **m**agic show complete with wand, hat, and cape.
- Watch a **m**agician.

Math Ideas:
- Teach the **m**onths of the year.
- Play a **m**atching game.
- Introduce **m**oney. Show and feel all different kinds of **m**oney (foreign or US). Research the history of **m**oney.

• Measure with a retractable tape **m**easure. **M**easure with liquids to 1/4 cup, 1/2 cup, 3/4 cups, pints, quarts, liters, etc.
• Count **M&M'S**™. Show how many zeroes are in a **m**illion. I recommend the book, *How Much Is A Million?* by David M Schwartz.
• Stay up until **m**idnight (or change clock to show midnight ☺).
• Do some **m**azes.

Science Ideas:
• Learn about **m**onkeys, **m**anatees, **m**ammals, or **m**oose.
• **M**ake **m**ud pies with nuts, leaves, rocks, acorns, and flower petals for decoration.
• Learn about **m**agma or **m**igration.
• Show the phases of the **m**oon using Oreos.

• Investigate **m**icroscopes. Observe a piece of hair, a thread, and a bug.
• **M**ake **m**old in or out of refrigerator using bread, sour cream, or old food.
• Experiment with **m**agnets: Help child spell word on refrigerator with letter **m**agnets or buy a kit. Kids love **m**agnets (parental supervision required; magnets are extremely dangerous if swallowed).
• **M**easure water or ingredients for a recipe using **m**easuring cups.
• **M**easure rainfall or snowfall.

Social Studies Ideas:
• Learn about the selflessness of **M**other Teresa.
• Learn about **M**orse code and Samuel **M**orse. See and hear Morse code online.
• **M**ake a **m**ummy: Wrap your child in toilet paper or **m**ummify a Barbie Doll™.
• Learn about **M**exico.
• Visit a **M**exican restaurant.
• Discover the history of the **M**arines.

Vocations: **M**agician, **m**aid, **m**ail carrier, **m**arine biologist, **m**assage therapist, **m**athematician, **m**echanic, **m**eteorologist, **m**ilitary, **m**issionary, **m**usician

Books:
• *Make Way for Ducklings* by Robert McCloskey
• *Mike Mulligan and His Steam Shovel* by Virginia Lee Burton
• *Milly-Molly-Mandy Storybook* by Joyce Lankester Brisley
• Mother Goose Rhymes

- *The Mitten* by Jan Brett
- *If You Give a Mouse a Cookie* by Laura Joffe Numeroff
- *Madeline* by Ludwig Bemelmans
- *Mirette on the High Wire* by Emily Arnold McCully

Music Appreciation:
Muzak, minuets

Composers: Henry Mancini, Felix Mendelssohn 1809–1847, Wolfgang Amadeus Mozart 1756–1791

Hymn: "Morning Has Broken"

Songs:
"She'll be Comin' Round the Mountain," "When the Saints Go Marching In," "The Bear Went Over the Mountain," "Three Blind Mice," "Michael Finnegan"

Movies to Watch: Malificent, *Monsters Inc.*, *Monsters University*, *Mary Poppins*, *Meet The Robinsons*, *Mickey Mouse*, *Mulan*, *The Muppets*, *March of The Penguins*, *Madagascar*, *Megamind*

Notes:

_____

_____

_____

_____

_____

_____

_____

The Letter N

 Sound : /n/ (no)

 Kinesthetic: Form letters out of play-dough, your body, or make letters outside from nature (sticks, leaves, petals, pinecones, etc.).

 Alphabet Notebook
• **Block Letter Pages:** Cut up a newspaper and glue onto your block letter **N**'s page.

• **Clip Art Pages:** Cut and paste clip art onto your **N**'s page.

 Handwriting Pages: Practice several upper and lower case letters every day this week.

 Menu Ideas:
Nachos, navel oranges, navy beans, Neapolitan ice-cream, New England clam chowder, New York strip steak, nectarines, noodles, northern beans, nuggets (chicken), nut bread, nuts (all kinds), Nutella™, Nutterbutter™ cookies

 Field Trip Ideas:
National Weather Service, nature walk, nature museum, newspaper tour, news station tour, or nursing home.

Bible Ideas:
Noah and the ark, the Nativity, Naboth, Nathan, Nazareth, Nebuchadrezzar, Nehemiah, Nicodemus

• **Missionary:** Nate Saint (1923–1956), Ecuador

Copy Work & Memory Verse: "No man can serve two masters..." (Matthew 6:24).

Character Traits: Nice, neat

Art:
- Make a **n**ecklace or bracelet with beads.
- Learn the art of **n**eedlepoint.
- Make a **n**oodle **n**ecklace. String dyed macaroni using food coloring and rubbing alcohol.
- Make **n**ecklace out of Cheerios™, Applejacks™, or Fruit Loops™, and then eat. Use tweezers to pick up items. This helps children with finger dexterity.
- Decorate paper **n**eckties.

Artist Study:
Norman Rockwell: Get a book from the library; kids love his comical paintings.

Poetry:
Read some of Ogden **N**ash's poems
The Best of Ogden Nash by Ogden **N**ash
Candy Is Dandy by Ogden **N**ash
The Tale of The Custard Dragon by Ogden **N**ash

Mother Goose:
NANCY DAWSON
Nancy Dawson was so fine
She wouldn't get up to serve the swine;
She lies in bed till eight or nine,
So it's Oh, poor Nancy Dawson.

And do ye ken Nancy Dawson, honey?
The wife who sells the barley, honey?
She won't get up to feed her swine,
And do ye ken Nancy Dawson, honey?

Activities:
- Make an edible **n**est out of butterscotch. Stir 1 can (or half a bag) of Chinese **n**oodles with a 12-oz. bag of melted butterscotch, and press into muffin tins. Use jelly beans or M&M'S™ as eggs.
- Discuss the **n**ewspaper: Show all the sections of the paper: local, sports, classifieds, movies, etc.
- Learn some simple **n**apkin-folding ideas. Have ready to use for dinner one **n**ight.
- Play a **n**ose game: Let child smell something sour, sweet, spicy, vanilla, cinnamon, chocolate, etc. without looking and see if child can detect smell.
- Taste different kinds of **n**uts.

- Buy or make a new **n**otebook for your child.
- Visit a **n**ursing home or start your own **n**ursing home ministry, http:// akahomeschoolmom.com/2012/how-to-start-a-nursing-home-ministry.
- Paint **n**ails with **n**ail polish. Do a **n**ail makeover: Clean, clip, and shine.
- Make **n**oise.
- Do something kind for your **n**eighbor.
- Using your child's **n**ame, make up encouraging and inspiring words for each letter.
- Make a paper hat out of **n**ewspaper.
- Discuss **n**ightmares.

Math Ideas:
- Write, trace, or color the **n**umbers 0–9.
- Count by fives using **n**ickels.
- Play **n**umber bingo.
- Draw a **n**umber line.
- Show and explain **n**egative **n**umbers.
- Show child that a **n**umerator is the top number of a fraction.

Science Ideas:
- Create a **n**ature journal if you haven't already.
- Learn about **n**arwhals.
- **N**utrition: Learn about food groups.
- Discover **n**octurnal animals.
- Find a **n**est or try to make one yourself. This will give you a greater appreciation for birds!
- Go on a **n**ature walk together.
- **N**ature walk scavenger hunt: Find 2 similar rocks, a stick, a large leaf, poison ivy, a yellow flower, a flying bug, a log, a pine cone, a bird, a bird's **n**est, a bird's feather, animal foot prints, a mushroom, an acorn, berries, a dandelion, etc.
- Make a **n**ature diorama.

Social Studies Ideas:
- Learn about Florence **N**ightingale or **N**eil Armstrong
- Discuss **n**atural resources—water soil, air, trees. See if your child can think of others.
- Learn about the **N**avy. Write a letter to someone in the **N**avy.

Vocations: **N**ational Guard, **N**avy, **n**eurologist, **n**ewscaster, **n**ewspaper reporter, TV news reporter, **n**un, **n**urse

Books:
- *The Best Nest* by P.D. Eastman

- *The Napping House* by Audrey and Don Wood
- *Too Much Noise* by Ann McGovern
- *A New Coat for Anna* by Harriet Ziefert
- *Noah's Ark* by Linda Hayward
- **Nursery Rhymes**

Music Appreciation:
- The **N**utcracker Suite- Dance of the Reed Flutes -Tchaikovsky
- **N**ature sounds in music (ocean waves, thunderstorms, running water, wind, and rain)
- **"N**ight of the Moonjellies" by Mark Shasha

Hymn: "**N**earer My God, To Thee"

Songs: "**N**obody Likes Me," "**N**inety Nine Bottles of Pop on The Wall," "The **N**ame Game Song"

Movies to Watch: *Nancy Drew, The Never Ending Story, The Chronicles of Narnia* (PG)

Notes:

_____

_____

_____

_____

_____

_____

_____

The Letter O

 Sound : /o/, /O/, /OO/ (ox, go, to)

 Kinesthetic: Form letters out of play-dough, your body, or make letters outside from nature (sticks, leaves, petals, pinecones, etc.).

 Alphabet Notebook
 • **Block Letter Pages:** Glue oatmeal or Cheerios™ onto your block letter O's page or color the Os orange.

• **Clip Art Pages:** Cut and paste clip art onto your O's page.

Handwriting Pages: Practice several upper and lower case letters every day this week.

 Menu Ideas:
Cheerios™, oatmeal, oatmeal cookies, octopus, okra, olive oil and bread, olives (black, green, Kalmata) , omelette, onion, onion rings, open-faced sandwiches, oolong tea, oranges, orange juice, orange marmalade, orange sherbet, orange sweet rolls, Oreos™, Oriental food, orzo, oysters, SpaghettiOs™

 Field Trip Ideas: Go to an observatory (tall building or planetarium). Go to an orchard (apple, blackberry, blueberry, peach, etc.).

 Bible Ideas:
Obadiah, Og, Onesimus, obedience, outdoors (where Jesus taught)
<u>One Another verses:</u> Accept one another; love one another; pray for one another; be patient with one another; help one another; do good things for one another; honor one another. Discuss how God is omnipotent, omnipresent, and omniscient.

Copy Work & Memory Verse: "O give thanks unto the Lord; He is good..." (Psalm 118:1).

Character Traits: Obedient, **o**bservant, **o**ptimistic, **o**rganized

Art:
• Make **o**rnaments. Pour paint into glass **o**rnament balls and swirl (careful not to mix colors too much or they will make a brown mess).
• Create paper **o**rnaments (Christmas tree, candy-cane, angel, shapes) and decorate with glitter. Glue popsicle sticks into a square or diamond, and put child's picture in center. Add a hanger.
• Learn **o**rigami. Get a book from the library.
• Make a picture with an **o**range crayon, **o**range pastel, **o**range paint, **o**range marker, or **o**range colored pencil (or all).
• Paint with **o**il paints.

Artist Study: **Georgia **O'Keeffe

Poetry:

Mother Goose:
OLD KING COLE
Old King Cole
Was a merry old soul,
And a merry old soul was he;
He called for his pipe,
And he called for his bowl,
And he called for his fiddlers three!
And every fiddler, he had a fine fiddle,
And a very fine fiddle had he.
"Twee tweedle dee, tweedle dee," went the fiddlers.
Oh, there's none so rare
As can compare
With King Cole and his fiddlers three.

Activities:
• Make an **o**wl puppet out of a paper bag.
• Make an **o**bstacle course using your child's or online ideas.
• Prepare something in an **o**ven or Easy Bake **O**ven™.
• Play **o**ffice: Use **o**ld telephone, junk mail, closet for an elevator, desk, pencil holder, chair, etc.
• Learn **o**pposites.
• Take child to get the **o**il changed in your car or teach them how to do it at home.
• String Cheerios™ on a string for a necklace. Then eat!
• Teach child how to make an **o**melette.
• Play **O**ld Maid.

- Sleep **o**vernight somewhere—grandparents, hotel, camping, etc.
- Discuss **o**besity.
- Discuss **o**bedience.
- Discuss **o**rganic.
- Ask your child for their **o**pinion on something. Discuss facts verses **o**pinions.
- Play **o**utside. "Kids who play on trees, rocks and uneven ground test better for motor fitness, balance and agility." Richard Louv (*Last Child in the Woods*)
- Go to an **o**cean if you have one near.
- **O**rganize a bookshelf, closet, cabinet, or drawer together.

Math Ideas:
- Draw **o**ctagons.
- Draw an **o**btuse angle.
- Show your child the **o**dometer on your car and explain what it counts.
- Teach **o**dd numbers with stuffed animals, showing how somebody is always left out without a buddy.
- Measure something in **o**unces or show a food item's weight in **o**unces on food packaging.

Science Ideas:
- Learn about **o**xygen in plants.
- Learn the meaning of an **o**mnivore.
- Learn about an **o**rbit: One person is the sun, one person is the earth, and one person is the moon. The earth orbits around the sun and spins while the orbiting the sun and the moon orbits around the earth as it is orbiting the sun.
- Learn about **o**wls, **o**ctopuses, or **o**tters.
- Make an **o**cean mural with real sand, seaweed, blue cellophane for water, cut-out fish, etc.
- **M**ake an ocean in a bottle.
- Peruse **o**ptical illusions.

Social Studies Ideas:
- Learn about the **O**lympics. Make a Jr. **O**lympics with competitions, such as a long jump, sprints, farthest throw, etc. Invite friends. Make the medals out of frozen juice can lids and ribbon.
- Discover and name the 5 **o**ceans of the Earth on a globe: Pacific **O**cean, Atlantic **O**cean, Indian **O**cean, Arctic **O**cean, and the Antarctic **O**cean.

Vocations: **O**ceanographer, **o**rthodontist, **o**perator, **o**bstetrician, **o**ptometrist

Books:
- *Ox-Cart Man* by Donald Hall
- *An Octopus Followed Me Home* by Dan Yaccarino

- *I Have an Olive Tree* by Eve Bunting
- *Paul Bunyan and His Blue Ox* by Patsy Jensen
- *Owl Moon* by Jane Yolen

Music Appreciation:
- Introduce your child to the **o**pera (go see one if you can, watch an opera online, or watch kids sing opera online).
- **O**riental Music, **o**rchestra music, **o**rgan music

Composers:
Jacques **O**ffenbach 1819–1880

Hymn: "**O** Little Town of Bethlehem" or "**O**nward Christian Soldiers"

Songs: "**O**ld McDonald Had a Farm," "**O**n Top **O**f **O**ld Smokey"

Movies to Watch: *Oliver and Company, Oliver Twist*

Notes:

_____

_____

_____

_____

_____

_____

_____

The Letter P

 Sound : /p/ (pan)

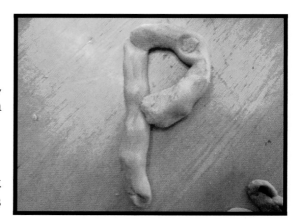

 Kinesthetic: Form letters out of play-dough, your body, or make letters outside from nature (sticks, leaves, petals, pinecones, etc.).

 Alphabet Notebook
• **Block Letter Pages:** **P**aint your **P**s **p**ink and **p**ur**p**le, or glue old **p**uzzle **p**ieces onto your block letter **P**'s page.

• **Clip Art Pages:** Cut and paste clip art onto your **P**'s page.

Pp **Handwriting Pages:** Practice several upper and lower case letters every day this week.

 Menu Ideas:
Pancake, **p**apaya, **p**armesan cheese, **p**assion fruit, **p**asta, **p**astrami, **p**astry, **p**each, **p**each cobbler, **p**eanuts, **p**eanut butter, **p**ear, **p**eas, **p**ecans, **p**epper jack cheese, **p**eppers (red, green, yellow), **P**eppermint **P**atties™, **p**epperoni, **P**epsi™, **p**erch, **p**ierogies, **p**ie, **p**ickles (dill, bread and butter), **p**ineapple, **p**ine nuts, **p**istachios, **p**ita chips, **p**izza, **p**lum, **P**olish sausage, **p**omegranate, **p**opcorn, **p**opsicles, **p**ork chops, **p**otatoes (baked, boiled, or mashed), **p**otato chips, **p**otato salad, **p**retzels (hard or soft), **p**rime rib, **P**ringles™, **p**udding, **p**umpernickel bread, **p**umpkin bread, **p**umpkin **p**ie, **p**umpkin seeds

 Field Trip Ideas:
Meet with a **p**hotographer and have your **p**icture taken. Go to a **p**et store, **p**lanetarium, **p**olice department tour, **p**ool (for swimming), **p**ost office for a tour, or a **p**ottery studio. Go to the **p**ound and rescue a **p**et. Go on a **p**ower **p**lant tour. Visit a **p**umpkin **p**atch. Meet a **p**lumber.

 Bible Ideas:
parable, **p**raise, **p**rayer, **P**aul, **P**eter, **p**haraoh, **P**hilemon, **P**hilip, **P**ilate, **P**otiphar, **P**riscilla

• **Missionary:** Paul The Apostle—Asia Minor and Europe (1st century world)

Copy Work & Memory Verse: "Praise ye the Lord: for it is good to sing praises unto our God" (Psalm 147:1).

Character Traits: Passionate, patience, peaceful, peacemaker, polite, punctual

Art:
• Just paint—oils, acrylics, or water colors.
• Make a picture with pastels (chalk or oil).

• Create and name a pet rock: Find a good smooth rock, add googly eyes, and paint. Put in small box with hay or straw.
• Make paper dolls.
• Pencil sketch using a pad and pencils.
• Learn how to do plastic canvas needlework.
• Craft a design with pipe cleaners.
• Make designs with pattern blocks. (These are a great investment.)
• Make a puppet out of a small lunch paper bag, socks, or wooden spoons, and have a puppet show.
• Paint concrete driveway with paintbrush and water. Practice letters.
• Make a pinata with paper mache (flour and water) or a pinata from a cardboard cereal box and decorate with tissue paper.
• Make a pinwheel.
• Make homemade purple play-dough or used store bought. Be sure to use tools—plastic knife, rolling pin, cookie cutter, and small toys.
• Make a placemat out of paper (any design your child may choose), and cover with contact paper for easy cleaning.
• Pressed nature. Ferns, flowers, leaves, or weeds—press between wax paper in a heavy phone book for a week or until completely dried. You can glue onto contact paper to make a placemat.
• Pirate treasure map: Use tea bags to stain paper then burn edges with wood burner to look old.
• Make a pencil holder: Cover sides of open vegetable or fruit can with construction paper, and decorate with pictures or stickers.
• Experiment with mixing paint—red and white = pink; red and blue= purple

Artist Study: Pablo Picasso (some of his paintings are not appropriate for young children). After seeing some of Picasso's paintings, have your child make his her own version of a Picasso.

Poetry:
Read Jack **P**relutsky's **p**oems
Something Big Has Been Here by Jack Prelutsky
Be Glad Your Nose Is on Your Face: and Other Poems Some of the Best of Jack Prelutsky by
Jack Prelutsky

Mother Goose:
PEASE **P**ORRIDGE
Pease porridge hot,
Pease porridge cold,
Pease porridge in the pot,
Nine days old.
Some like it hot,
Some like it cold,
Some like it in the pot,
Nine days old.

 Activities:
- Have a **p**ajama day and wear **p**ajamas all day.
- Go to a **p**lay or **p**retend you are in one.
- Discuss **p**ollution.
- **P**lay.

• Make homemade **p**opsicles using juice. Take small paper cups, fill with juice, use **p**opsicle sticks for handle and freeze.
• Carve a **p**umpkin with your child (parental supervision required).
• Play Pick-up Sticks™.
• **P**lay **p**ing-**p**ong.
• Ride in a **p**ickup truck.
• Find **p**ill bugs under rocks. Hold them.
• Walk on a **p**ier.
• Have a **p**illow fight.
• Give child a **p**iggy back ride.
• Teach the **p**eace symbol with your hands.
• Have a **p**icnic.
• Raid the recyclables and have a **p**aper ball fight.
• Make up a **p**oem using, "Roses are red, Violets are blue..."
• Ask child to **p**ray **p**ublicly.
• **P**ack for a trip—real or pretend, near or far.
• **P**olish something together (silver, shoes, etc.).
• Watch **p**antomime.
• Teach your child how to **p**ay for something.
• **P**lan a **p**arty.

- Take care of a **p**et. Ideally, have your child responsible for their own **p**et, whether it is a dog, hamster, or a hermit crab.
- Smell **p**erfume.
- **P**eel **p**otatoes with a **p**eeler.
- Make a **p**aper airplane.
- Enjoy **p**oetry. Memorize some easy **p**oems.
- Order **p**izza.
- Make homemade **p**izza with English muffin, **p**izza dough, or biscuit, **p**izza sauce, mozzarella cheese, and **p**epperoni.
- Explain **p**oison. Discuss the National **P**oison Center (http://www.poison.org/home.asp) and the phone number.
- Collect **p**ennies.
- Study **p**alindromes—race car, eye, mom, dad, Hannah, kayak, never odd or even, etc.
- Make a **p**ie.
- Identify **p**oison ivy.
- Make homemade or microwave **p**opcorn.
- Mail a **p**ostcard to a relative or friend. (Glue picture to card stock to make one.)
- Watch a **p**arade.
- Have a **p**arade of bikes on your street. Get neighbors involved. Don't forget streamers!
- Grow **p**arsley or use in your dinner.
- Memorize the **P**ledge of Allegiance, how to stand and cover your heart, and learn about its history.

- Watch Red Skelton's **P**ledge of Allegiance on-line.
- Do school on your **p**atio.
- Show your child a **p**assport.
- Learn the **p**arts of speech. Teach child *verbs* by having them do something (jumping, swinging, hanging, etc.). Teach *nouns* by having them hold something (rocks, snails, leaves, etc.). Teach *adjectives* by describing what they are holding (hard, slimy, green, etc.).
- Watch a **p**uppet show. Discover Japanese Bunraku **p**uppets.
- Have your own **p**uppet show **p**erformance. Use a spring-loaded curtain rod in a doorway.
- Listen to a **p**arrot talk.
- Do a **p**uzzle. Start with small easy **p**uzzles. Make your own **p**uzzle.
- **P**icnic at the **p**ark.
- Make a string **p**hone with cans and a taut string; then talk to each other.

 Math Ideas:
- Learn how to make **p**atterns with numbers, colors, or shapes.
- Use **p**attern blocks and have child copy a **p**attern you make. Reverse.
- Using numbers or shapes, make a simple **p**attern and have child finish it. For example: 1, 1, 2, 1 or triangle, circle, square, etc.
- Learn about **p**olygons.

- Draw a **p**olygon.
- Make a simple **p**ie chart of your child's day (12 hours spent sleeping, 2 hours of school, 2 hours of eating, 3 hours of **p**laying, etc.).
- Draw **p**arallel lines, **p**arenthesis, and a **p**ercent (%) symbol.
- Discuss **p**robability: "It is very **p**robable that you will be in bed at 8 o'clock tonight." Probability of a coin toss—50% heads, 50% tails.
- Patterns: Cut red straws into **p**ieces; use beads, buttons, and make **p**atterns for child to make or copy onto a string.

Science Ideas:
- Learn about the **p**anda bear.
- Study the **p**lanets.
- Perform **p**ine cone experiments: **P**ut in oven and watch open; put in freezer and watch it close up tight.
- Drop **p**ennies into a shot glass placed at the bottom of a large jar or container of water.
- Learn about a **p**lant's anatomy.
- Learn about **p**iranhas.
- Make a **p**ine cone bird feeder.

Social Studies Ideas:
- Study the **P**ilgrims.
- Discover **P**ocohontas and what she did.
- Locate the **P**acific Ocean on a map.
- What did Rosa **P**arks do?
- Look at all of America's **p**residents.
- Discuss **p**rejudice.
- Draw a **p**yramid. Show pictures of Egyptian **p**yramids.

Vocations: Painter, **p**aralegal, **p**aramedic, **p**ark ranger, **p**astor, **p**ediatrician, **p**et store owner, **p**harmacist, **p**hotographer, **p**hysicist, **p**ianist, **p**ilot, **p**olice officer, **p**lumber, **p**resident, **p**rofessional athlete, **p**sychologist, **p**sychiatrist, **p**uppeteer

Books:
- *The Story About Ping* by Marjorie Flack and Kurt Wiese
- *The Complete Adventures of Peter Rabbit*
- *Please and Thank You Book* by Richard Scarry
- *The Poky Little Puppy* by Janette Sebring Lowrey
- *Play With Me* by Marie Hall Ets
- *Prayer for a Child* by Rachel Field
- *Papa Piccolo* by Carol Talley

Music Appreciation:
Polka, pop, praise music, patriotic music, piano solos

 Composers:
Sergei Prokofiev 1891–1953, Giacomo Puccini 1858–1924, Henry Purcell 1659–1695, Johann Pachelbel 1653–1706. Listen to "Canon in D major."

 Hymn: "Praise Him! Praise Him!"

 Songs: "Found a Peanut," "Polly Put the Kettle On," "Peanut Sat on A Railroad Track"

 Movies to Watch: *Pinnochio, Peter Pan, **Pippi** Longstocking, Planes, Pocohontas, Pollyanna, Pooh's Grand Adventure, Puss 'n Boots*

Notes:

_____

_____

_____

_____

_____

_____

_____

_____

The Letter Q

 Sound : /kw/ (queen)

 Kinesthetic: Form letters out of play-dough, your body, or make letters outside from nature (sticks, leaves, petals, pinecones, etc.).

 Alphabet Notebook
• **Block Letter Pages:** Cut up old fabric and glue pieces onto your block letter **Q**'s page (to resemble a patchwork **q**uilt), or glue **Q**-tips or **Q**-tips pieces inside your **Q**s.

• **Clip Art Pages:** Cut and paste clip art onto your **Q**'s page.

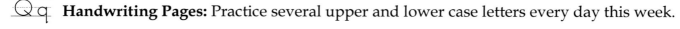 **Handwriting Pages:** Practice several upper and lower case letters every day this week.

 Menu Ideas: Quail, **q**uiche, **Q**uiznos™ subs, **Q**uaker Oats™, **q**uarter bread pudding, **q**uesadillas, **q**uiche, **q**uick bread, **q**uinoa

 Field Trip Ideas: A rock **q**uarry, **q**uilting club, or **q**uiver (archery)

 Bible Ideas:
Queen Esther, **Q**ueen Jezebel, **Q**ueen of Sheba, **Q**uartus, **q**uestions (Jesus often answered **q**uestions with **q**uestions)

Copy Work & Memory Verse: "**Q**uicken me after thy lovingkindness; so shall I keep the testimony of thy mouth" (Psalm 119:88).

Character Traits: Quick, **q**uiet

Art:
- **Q**-tip paint with a **Q**-tip for a brush.
- Draw a **q**ueen.
- Try crazy **q**uilting with paper or fabric.

• Buy or make a **q**uill pen out of a feather, and write with it (take apart a pen and stick the ink piece into a feather).
• Draw a **q**uilt on a piece of paper and have child color each square a different color.

Poetry:

Mother Goose:
THE **Q**UARREL
My little old man and I fell out;
I'll tell you what 'twas all about,—
I had money and he had none,
And that's the way the noise begun.

Activities:
- Measure a **q**uart.
- Pretend to be a **q**ueen and make a crown out of cardboard, aluminum foil, and craft jewels.
- Make a **q**uarter rubbing with the side of a crayon or a pencil.

• Have a **q**uiet time.
• Show your child a real **q**uilt.
• **Q**uiver.
• **Q**uickly, play Hot Potato.
• **Q**uickly, run around the house.
• Discuss the definition of **q**uarrel. Pretend to have one or bring up the fact that someone is **q**uarreling this week.
• Watch the **q**uickstep dance.
• Learn about **q**uestion marks and have your child copy or trace one.
• Use **q**uiet inside voices as opposed to loud outside voices.
• Play the **Q**uiet Game (see who can go without talking the longest).
• Play the **Q**ueen Clean-up Game. One person pretends to be the **q**ueen and instructs her subject to pick up three things. Then the next child pretends to be **q**ueen and repeats.
• Go on a **q**uest for something.
• Give an oral **q**uiz on something you have been learning.
• Learn how to play **q**uarterback.
• Type up a small **q**uestionnaire and write answers for your child: 1. What is your favorite color? 2. What do you want to be when you grow up? 3. What is your favorite food? 4. What is your favorite thing to do? 5. Where is your favorite place to go? 6. What is your favorite book? 7. If you could have one super power, what would it be? etc.

Math Ideas:
- **Q**uarters: Count with **q**uarters by 25 to 100 or 200
- Divide hours or food into **q**uarters (1/4).
- Draw a **q**uadrilateral.
- Discuss that a **q**uotient is the answer to a division problem. If there are 8 cookies and 4 kids, divide 8 by 4, and the quotient or answer is 2. (The idea is to become familiar with the word and concept, not to understand it in its entirety.)
- Flip a **q**uarter 50 times. Guess how many times it will land on heads.

Science Ideas:
- **Q**uack like a duck; learn about ducks in your area.
- Discuss **q**uadruplets.
- Show your child **q**uartz rock.
- Learn about a **q**uasar.
- Learn about the **q**ueen bee from a real bee keeper if you are able.
- Learn about **q**uicksand.

Social Studies Ideas:
- Learn about famous **q**ueens in history—the **Q**ueen of England or **Q**ueen Cleopatra.
- Tell about the **Q**ing dynasty.
- Find out about **Q**uakers.
- Find **Q**uebec, Canada on a map.

Vocations: **Q**uartermaster, **q**uality control inspector, **q**uantum physicist, **q**uarterback, **q**ueen

Books:
- *Quick, Quack, Quick!* by Marsha Arnold
- *The Josefina Story Quilt* by Eleanor Coerr
- *Quick as a Cricket* by Audrey Wood
- *The Quiet Way Home* by Bonny Becker

Music Appreciation:
Listen to a **q**uartet champion or a teen **q**uartet,
Discuss a **q**uarter note.

Hymn: "**Q**uiet, Lord, My Froward Heart"

Movies to Watch: *Quest for Camelot* (may be too scary for some children, see review), Watch **Q**uasimoto from *Hunchback of Notre Dame*

Notes:

_____

_____

_____

_____

_____

_____

_____

_____

_____

The Letter R

 Sound : /r/ (ran)

 Kinesthetic: Form letters out of play-dough, your body, or make letters outside from nature (sticks, leaves, petals, pinecones, etc.).

 Alphabet Notebook
• **Block Letter Pages:** Glue pieces of **r**ibbon or **r**ice (can color with food coloring and shake in a baggie) onto your block letter **R**'s page.

• **Clip Art Pages:** Cut and paste clip art onto your **R**'s page.

 Handwriting Pages: Practice several upper and lower case letters every day this week.

Menu Ideas:
Radish, **R**agu Sauce™, rainbow sherbet, rainbow trout, **R**aisin Bran™ cereal, raisins, **R**amen™ noodles, ranch dressing and veggies, raspberries, ratatouille, ravioli, red jello, red onion, red potatoes, **R**eese's Pieces™, relish, **R**euben sandwich, rhubarb, ribeye steak, ribs, rice, rice cakes, ricotta cheese, rice pudding, **R**ice Krispies™ cereal, **R**ice Krispy™ treats, risotto, **R**itz Crackers™, roast beef, rocky road ice-cream, **R**ollos™ candies, rolls, romaine lettuce, root beer, rosemary, **R**uffles™ potato chips, rutabagas, rye bread

 Field Trip Ideas: Go to a **r**ace (car, dog, horse, marathon); go see a **r**ace car; tour a **r**adio station, **r**aptor center, or a **r**ecycling plant tour. Enjoy a **R**enaissance festival. Go **r**ock climbing. Watch a **r**ock concert. Attend a **r**odeo. Meet a **r**eal estate broker. Go out to eat at a new **r**estaurant. Go **r**oller skating.

Bible Ideas:
The story of **R**achel, **R**ebekah, **R**ehab, **R**ehobam, **R**euben, **R**hoda, **R**uth, **r**esurrection of Christ, the **R**oman Empire; Discover God's promise to mankind through a **r**ainbow.

• **Missionary: R**owland Bingham (1872–1942), Africa

Copy Work & Memory Verse: "**R**emember the Sabbath day, to keep it holy." (Exodus 20:8)

Character Traits: Rejoicing, **r**eliable, **r**esourceful, **r**espectful, **r**esponsible, **r**everent, The Golden **R**ule

 Art:
• Draw **r**abbits.
• Color a **r**ainbow: ROYGBIV (red, orange, yellow, green blue, indigo, violet).
• **R**ainbow **r**ain: Put large watery drops of different color paint with a paint brush at top of piece of paper, and then hold vertical on an easel encouraging drops to drip and run down paper.
• Try **r**ubber stamping with **r**ubber stamps and an ink pad.
• **R**ainbow **R**ice: Take 2 teaspoons of **r**ubbing alcohol, a good amount of food coloring and about 3 4 cup of **r**ice in a Ziploc™ bag and shake. Let dry on cookie sheet. Glue onto your **R** or make pretty pictures with your **r**ainbow **r**ice. (Food coloring can stain clothes.)
• **R**ubbings: Using the side of a crayon, **r**ub leaves, coins, keys, paper clips, safety pins, etc.
• Make a coffee filter **r**ose.
• Make a **r**eindeer—upside down footprint for head and one handprint for antlers (at heel of footprint). Draw eyes and nose.

Artist Study: Rembrandt, Norman **R**ockwell

 Poetry:
Read Christina **R**ossetti's poems.
Sing-Song: A Nursery Rhyme Book by Christina **R**ossetti
The Complete Poems by Christina **R**ossetti

Mother Goose:
RAIN
Rain, rain, go away,
Come again another day;
Little Johnny wants to play.

 Activities:
• Have **r**ecess.

- **R**est.
- **R**ide a **r**iding lawnmower.
- Play a **r**ecorder.
- Listen to the **r**adio.
- Make **r**ock candy.
- **R**oller-skate at a **r**ink or in your driveway.
- Play in the **r**ain with **r**ain boots and an umbrella.
- Pretend to be a **r**obot.
- **R**ock child in a **r**ocking chair.
- Use a **r**olling pin to **r**oll play-dough.
- **R**ake leaves in a pile and JUMP!
- Share a **r**ock collection. Start a **r**ock collection.
- Have child **r**ace with his friends.
- Play **r**acquetball.

- Make a **r**outine. Our children's morning **r**outine consists of: Make bed, eat breakfast, brush teeth, get dressed, and brush hair. I laminated a little chart with pictures of these five activities and hung it for my children to see every morning.
- Make a **r**epair shop: Take apart real life things to make **r**eal life puzzles. For example, give kids a flashlight to try. Then take it completely apart—batteries bulb, etc. Then let child attempt to put back together.
- Buy or grow **r**oses. Put on kitchen table to enjoy.
- **R**ecycle. Make separate containers for paper and plastic.
- Save **r**ecyclables and build something (use cardboard boxes, tubes, cans, plastic, etc.).
- **R**oll ball into empty bucket or empty trashcan (on its side) as a game, or roll a ball to each other.
- Borrow a kid's cookbook from the library and let child choose a **r**ecipe. Then help them make the **r**ecipe.
- **R**ead a book.
- Buy or make a **r**ain gauge and measure after it **r**ains.
- Play **R**ed Light Green Light.

Math Ideas:
- Draw **r**ectangles: Trace, draw, and find objects around you that are **r**ectangles.
- Explain **r**adius.
- Draw a **r**hombus. Encourage child to copy it.
- Measure with a **r**uler.
- Draw a **r**ay.
- Show some **R**oman numerals and places (like books) where they are used.
- Teach a **r**ight angle. Draw a simple **r**ight triangle.

Science Ideas:
• **R**ainbow in a jar: Fill large jar 2/3 full of water and pour a small layer of oil on top of water (about 1–2 cm; the more oil, the longer for the color to explode through). Drop food coloring drops of different colors on top of oil. Try to get a couple drops in the same spot. The food coloring will press through the oil and explode into the water. It is beautiful!
• Learn about **r**abies, **r**attlesnakes, **r**abbits, **r**hinoceroses, or **r**eindeer.
• Catch **r**oly polies.
• Make **r**ock candy.
• Discover **r**ocks, **r**obotics, **r**ain forests, or **r**ockets.
• **R**esearch **r**ainbows.
• Try a **r**ocket experiment with an old film canister and an Alka Seltzer™.

 Social Studies Ideas:
• Read about Eleanor **R**oosevelt
• Learn about the **R**evolutionary War.
• Briefly discuss different **r**eligions.
• Discuss **r**ules and laws.
• Read about **R**ome.
• Learn about **r**ecycling.
• Learn about **R**ussia.
• Go to a **R**ussian food store and buy food for dinner.

 Vocations: Race car driver, **r**adio DJ, **r**eal estate agent, **r**ecreational therapist, **r**eferee, **r**egistered nurse, **r**epairman, **r**eporter, **r**estaurant manager, **r**everend, **r**oofer, **r**ock climber

 Books:
• *Rain* by Robert Kalan
• *A Pair of Red Clogs* by Masako Matsuno
• *The Rag Coat* by Lauren Mills Round Robin by Jack Kent
• *Little Red Riding Hood* retold by Harriet Ziefert
• *The Rainbow Fish* by Marcus Pfister
• *The Red Carpet* by Rex Parkin
• *The Runaway Bunny* by Margaret Wise Brown
• *Miss Rumphius* by Barbara Cooney

 Music Appreciation:
Reggae music

Composers:
Sergei **R**achmaninoff 1873–1943, Nikolai **R**imsky-Korsakov 1844–1908, Joaquín **R**odrigo 1901–1999, Gioachino **R**ossini 1792–1868,

Hymn: "**R**ock of Ages"

Songs:
"I've Been Working on the **R**ailroad"
"**R**ow, **R**ow, **R**ow Your Boat"

Movies to Watch:
Ratatouille, The Rescuers, Robin Hood

Notes:

_____

_____

_____

_____

_____

_____

The Letter S

 Sound : /s/, /z/ (sit, as)

 Kinesthetic: Form letters out of play-dough, your body, or make letters outside from nature (sticks, leaves, petals, pinecones, etc.).

 Alphabet Notebook
• **Block Letter Pages:** Glue seeds, sand, or put stickers on your block letter **S**'s page. Stamp inside your **Ss**. Or cut **Ss** out of sandpaper.

• **Clip Art Pages:** Cut and paste clip art onto your **S**'s page.

S̄s̄ **Handwriting Pages:** Practice several upper and lower case letters every day this week.

 Menu Ideas:
Salad, salami, salmon, salsa, salt, sandwiches, sardines, sauerkraut, sausage, scallops, scampi, scrambled eggs, seafood, shrimp, sirloin, Skittles™, Sloppy Joes™, Smarties™ candies, smoked fish, s'mores, soufflé, soup, sour cream, sourdough bread, spaghetti, spaghetti sauce, Spam™, spinach, squash, Starburst™ candy, steak, stew, strawberries, strawberry jelly, strawberry shortcake, string beans, string cheese, stroganoff, Stromboli, stuffing, sugar, sugar cane (real sugar cane—taste and eat!), sugar cookies, sugar cubes, SunChips™, sunflower seeds, sushi (you can get veggie sushi at the grocery store), Swedish meatballs, sweet and sour pork chicken, sweet potatoes, sweet tea, Swiss roll, swordfish, syrup

 Field Trip Ideas:
Visit a sanitary landfill, science fair, or science museum. Meet a scuba diver or a scientist. Tour the sheriff's office. Go swimming. Go to the state fair. Go hear a storyteller.

 Bible Ideas:
Samson and Delilah, Samuel, Saul, Seth, Shadrach, Simeon, Solomon, Stephen Discuss the Sabbath; read Sermon on the Mount.

• **Missionary:** Saint Patrick, Ireland (study the history of St. Patrick's Day)

Copy Work & Memory Verse: "Seek ye the Lord while He may be found..." (Isaiah 55:6).

Character Traits: Self-control, self-discipline, sensitive, sincere

Art:
• Create paper snowflakes.
• Mix shaving cream and paint and then paint.
• Create a snow picture: Cotton balls, white paint, on dark blue or black paper; use upside down triangles cut out of foil for icicles to hang on branches.
• Create scribble art.
• Make a silhouette of your child.
• Create a scrapbook with your child with photos, stamps, and stickers.
• Create a scrapbook of leaves, feathers, and other things she/he finds in nature.
• Build a snowman out of snow or sand.
• Make salt dough.
• Attach streamers to a straw and dance like no one's watching!
• Symmetrical art: Put blob of paint on paper, fold in half, smoosh, and then open to reveal symmetrical art.
• Draw or paint a tree in all four seasons. Play Vivaldi's "Four Seasons" while you and your child create.
• Straw Painting: Put watery paint blobs on paper, and let child blow on the paint through a straw. It makes delightful designs.
• Make a sewing card: Take a paper plate, draw a picture, use a hole puncher to make holes. Use yarn and a plastic sewing needle to sew the card. Or print sewing cards free online.
• Teach your child to sew by hand. Find an easy felt pattern, sew, and stuff with stuffing.
• Create Shrinky Dinks™.

Poetry:
Read Shel Silverstein poems
Falling Up by Shel Silverstein
Where The Sidewalk Ends by Shel Silverstein
The Missing Piece by Shel Silverstien
Read some of Carl Sandburg's poems online.
Poetry For Young People: Carl Sandburg by Carl Sandburg

Mother Goose:
SING A SONG OF SIXPENCE
Sing a song of sixpence,
A pocket full of rye;
Four-and-twenty blackbirds
Baked in a pie!

When the pie was opened
The birds began to sing;
Was not that a dainty dish
To set before the king?

The king was in his counting-house,
Counting out his money;
The queen was in the parlor,
Eating bread and honey.

The maid was in the garden,
Hanging out the clothes;
When down came a blackbird
And snapped off her nose.

 Activities:
• Balance a spoon on your nose!
• Storybook stew: Start a story, have your child add a line or two, then add some more to story, and let your child finish. Lots of fun with multiple kids.
• Learn some basic sign language.
• Sign Language "I Love You" Handprint: Trace child's hand, fold down 2 fingers to form "I love You" in sign language. (Great for Valentine's Day.)
• Slide on a slide.
• Snuggle.
• Stretch.
• Match socks from the dryer.
• Discuss how to treat a sunburn.
• Play soccer or learn to kick a soccer ball.
• Shadow dancing on the wall or watch this hand shadow car commercial.
(https://www.youtube.com/watch?v=e0UBuDI0mUc)
• Shaving cream: Play in tub during bath time.
• Enjoy the sun.
• Play sprinkler games.

- Slip on a Slip-n-Slide.™
- Allow your child to pick out a pair of UV protection sunglasses.
- Have your child tell you the speed limit when you drive. Start teaching by pointing out speed limit signs and other street signs.
- Perform a somersault.
- Sing a song.
- Play in a sand box. (You can also fill a large plastic container with sand and measuring cups.)
- Buy burlap sacks from a local hardware store and have sack races. We have used ours for years.
- Enjoy a seashell collection. Sort seashells and learn the names.
- Start a stamp collection.
- Scramble eggs.
- Teach stranger safety tips to your child.
- Play string games.
- Eat nutritious snacks. Discuss why the snack is nutritious.
- Go sledding.
- Make a shadow box.
- Wear a scarf. Learn how to wear a scarf.
- Splash in the tub or pool. Allow child to have a splash party in the tub. Then show child how to clean it up.
- Snorkel in the tub.
- Build a sandcastle or sand sculpture.
- Swing.
- Skip.
- Eat something sour (like a slice of lemon) and capture your child's "sour face."
- Try something spicy.
- Be a Salvation Army bell ringer volunteer.
- Smell essential oils—cinnamon, vanilla, pine, etc.
- Tell your child a secret.
- Play Simon Says.
- Watch a skydiver skydive on-line.
- Watch a sunrise and sunset.
- Screw a screw into a piece of wood with a screwdriver.
- Move in slow motion.
- Explain why smoking is bad for you.
- Have a smorgasbord of "S" foods.
- Set the table together.
- Teach your child how to sweep the floor.
- Skype™ a friend or family member.
- Watch a sunrise and sunset.

Math Ideas:

• Look at different shapes. Pattern blocks are great for this and are a good investment.
• Draw shapes: Draw a scalene triangle. Draw a square. Trace some shapes. Cut shapes out of sandpaper, scrap fabric, or felt.
• Teach how to subtract by sharing.
• Sort something — nuts and bolts, buttons, candy.
• Count Skittles™.
• Introduce symmetry using paint or a mirror on an object

Science Ideas:

• Read about squirrels, swans, snakes, or sloths.
• Try using a stethoscope to listen to sounds of the heart and tummy (caution children not to be loud while using a stethoscope).
• Name some bones on a skeleton.
• Discuss spring and summer.
• Discuss the 5 senses (sight, smell, sound, touch, taste).
• Read about the stars and the sun in our solar system.
• Learn about solar energy.
• Make slime (parental supervision: messy, may stain). Get the recipe on-line.
• Plant seeds and watch them grow.
• Learn about sea snakes, the sea horse, sea urchins, or sea cucumbers.
• Preserve a spider web with black construction paper, hairspray, and spray paint.
• Play with Silly Putty™; pick up newsprint with it.

Social Studies Ideas:
• Learn about Spain.
• Learn a dozen or more words, a song, and how to say "hello" and "goodbye" in Spanish.

• Briefly discuss slavery: the institution that supports the holding of human beings as property.
• Learn the history about the Statue of Liberty.
• Study steam engines.
• Read something from William Shakespeare or discuss words he invented or phrases he coined such as: "As luck would have it," "Neither a borrower or a lender be," "A heart of gold," "In a pickle," etc.
• Discuss the stock market when you see it on the nightly news.
• Start a savings account at a bank or at home. Whenever your child receives money, teach them how to tithe 10% first, then save 10%, then spend the rest if they choose. There is a My Giving Bank™ you can use for this or just label 3 containers for tithing, savings, spending.
• Sponsor a child with Compassion™.

Vocations: Sailor, salesman, sand sculptor, scientist, scuba diver, secretary, seamstress, silversmith, singer, soldier, song writer, speech pathologist, social worker, software developer, sound designer, sports announcer, statistician, storyteller, surgeon

Books:
- *Snowy Day* by Ezra Jack Keats
- *Sand Castle* by Brenda Shannon Yea
- *The Seashore Book* by Charlotte Zolotow
- *Snow* by Roy McKie and P.D. Eastman
- *Stopping by Woods on a Snowy Evening* by Robert Frost (with illustrations by Susan Jeffers)
- *Stone Soup* by Marcia Brown
- *The Snowy Day* by Ezra Jack Keats

Music Appreciation:
Salsa, symphonic, square dancing, songs of the sixties and seventies

Composers:
Franz Schubert 1797–1828, John Philip Sousa 1854–1932, Richard Strauss 1864–1949, Johann Strauss Jr. 1825–1899, Igor Stravinsky 1882–1971

Hymn: "Standing on the Promises"

Songs:
Sing silly songs: "I'm a Nut," "Bazooka Bubblegum Song," "Boom Boom Ain't It Great To Be Crazy," "Do Your Ears Hang Low?," "Found a Peanut," "Lemon Drop," "Little Bunny Foo-Foo," "Ten in the Bed," "Great Green Globs," "Sesame Street Theme Song"

Movies to Watch:
The Santa Clause, The Shaggy Dog, Sleeping Beauty, Snow White, The Swan Princess, Swiss Family Robinson, Scooby Doo movies or episodes (I do not recommend the newer non-animated ones)

The Letter T

 Sound : /t/ (tap)

 Kinesthetic: Form letters out of play-dough, your body, or make letters outside from nature (sticks, leaves, petals, pinecones, etc.).

 Alphabet Notebook
• **Block Letter Pages:** Glue toothpicks onto your block letter Ts. Or make your Ts out of toothpicks. Glue tinsel or draw triangles inside your Ts. Tear pieces of tissue paper (colored) and glue onto your T's page.

• **Clip Art Pages:** Cut and paste clip art onto your T's page.

Handwriting Pages: Practice several upper and lower case letters every day this week.

 Menu Ideas:
Tabouli, tacos, taffy, tamales, tangerines, tapioca pudding, tarts, tater-tots, T-bone steak, tea (hot or cold), Teddy Grahams™, tempura, tenderloin, teriyaki chicken, tilapia, tiramisu (Italian dessert), toast, toffee, tofu, tomato, Tootsie Roll™, tortellini, tortilla chips, Total™ cereal, Trident™ gum, Triscuits™, trout, truffles, tuna fish, turkey, turkey pot pie, turnips, turtle cheesecake, Twix™ candy bar, Twizzlers™

 Field Trip Ideas: Go to a marine touch tank. Go to the theater (or schedule a tour). Try different transportation (subway, metro, linx, train, bus, etc.). Visit a train station. Ride in a taxi. Meet a taxidermist. Do a TV station tour. Check out 18 wheeler trucks.

 Bible Ideas:
The temptation of Christ, Ten Commandments, ten lepers, tithing Tamar, Terah, doubting Thomas, Tobiah, Timothy, Titus

Copy Work & Memory Verse: "Trust in the Lord with all your heart and lean not on your own understanding" (Proverbs 3:5).

Character Traits: Thankful, thoughtful, trustworthy, truthful

Art:
• Tissue blossoms: Cut tissue paper into small squares of different colors. Using the eraser of a pencil in center of square, glue to paper in a pattern of flowers.
• Draw tulips.
• Tie-dye a t-shirt.
• Decorate a t-shirt with fabric paint. Have children's friends sign your child's t-shirt in permanent ink.
• Make a treasure box.
• Experiment with trick photography.
• Toothpick Punch Art:
Materials: Tea or hand towel, black construction paper cut in half, toothpicks, white paper cut in half, marker, two clothespins.
Instructions: Draw simple shapes with a wide marker on white paper. Using the tea towel as a pad, layer the materials, towel, black construction paper, white "pattern," and secure with clothespins. Poke holes with the toothpick along the marked lines. Discard the white paper. Hold the black paper up to the window to see the outline created.
• Discover tatting.
• Learn the basics of tole painting.

Poetry:

Mother Goose:
THE TEN O'CLOCK SCHOLAR
A diller, a dollar, a ten o'clock scholar!
What makes you come so soon?
You used to come at ten o'clock,
But now you come at noon.

Activities:
• Play tennis on a tennis court with tennis balls.
• Make a time capsule.
• Buy tickets to something, or give out tickets each time Bible verse is said correctly and then award a prize.
• Climb a tree.
• Teach child how to clean a toilet (make sure child washes hands).
• Have a tea party.
• Have a teddy bear tea party, complete with treats.
• Wear a toboggan.
• Play tag.
• Play with tangrams. Make your own tangrams.

- Speak to grandparents (or other loved ones) on the telephone.
- Learn telephone manners: How to answer the phone and how to take a message.
- Fold towels (easiest for kids to fold).
- Teach child to blow nose into a tissue.
- Put a tablecloth on the table for a special dinner.
- Ride a tricycle.
- Make a tee-pee (small or big).
- Make a tower with blocks or other stackable items.
- Make a treasure box. Paint a box and decorate with pasta, jewels, sticks, etc.
- Trace shapes—circle, square, rectangle, triangle, trapezoid, hexagon.
- Trace using a light box.
- Play a tambourine.
- Talk. I find this is great to do when cooking dinner.
- Take a timeout.
- Teach the color meanings of a traffic light.
- Show child where the turn signal is on cars as you drive around town.
- Look through a telescope.
- Make a telescope using toilet paper and paper towel tubes.
- Watch a rocket take off.
- Teach child how to brush their teeth. Allow child to choose a new toothbrush.
- Let your child teach you something.
- Travel on a train, a trolley, or a taxi-cab.
- Play tag.
- Visit your town hall.
- Teach child how to check their body temperature (parental supervision with thermometers).
- Jump on a trampoline.
- Trade something with friends or siblings.
- Practice checking the outside and inside temperatures.
- Target practice with balls, darts, or bean bags.
- Take apart something and put it back together.
- Go to a theater.
- Listen to a Christian testimony.
- Ride a tractor.
- Build a tent.
- Read a book about trucks.
- Attempt tae kwon do.
- Make homemade taffy.
- Share a Tic-Tac™.
- Have a taste test—sour, sweet, spicy, bland, etc.
- Hug a teacher.
- Learn how to tie a tie.
- Play Tiddlywinks™.
- Watch a turtle at a pet store or buy a turtle as a pet.
- Discover tongue twisters.

Math Ideas:
- Measure with a fabric tape measure or a retractable tape measure.
- Measure with tablespoons and teaspoons (showing the difference) and introduce the abbreviations (T., t., 1, 1/2, 1/4, 1/8).
- Introduce time: a.m. vs. p.m., o'clocks, quarters of an hour, 1/2 hour.
- Draw triangles and trapezoids.
- Show how many zeros are in a trillion. (There are twelve—1,000,000,000,000).
- Discuss twice and triple.
- Teach tally marks with candy, pennies, or something you count.
- Discuss total.
- Make a square, triangle, and rectangle out of toothpicks.

Science Ideas:
- Learn about tigers, turtles, or toucans.
- Learn about ticks and how to prevent them.
- Watch tornados on YouTube.
- Create a tornado in a jar using a jar, water, dish washing liquid, and vinegar.
- Use a tree identification book in your backyard, neighborhood, or a nearby park. Your child should be able to identify several types of trees.
- Read about teeth.
- Look through a telescope.
- Watch the development of a tadpole into a frog.
- Watch a tidal wave on YouTube in China (May be too mature for your child, so preview first).
- Learn about tsunamis.
- Go to a touch tank.
- Watch a tarantula.
- Watch a Tasmanian devil (not for the squeamish).

Social Studies Ideas:
- Learn the history of the teddy bear and Theodore Roosevelt.
- Read about Harriet Tubman.
- Introduce traffic signs either in traffic as you ride together or set up/draw with chalk pretend signs on your driveway as your kids and their friends ride tricycles, scooters, and bikes.
- Learn about different types of transportation.
- Explain the meaning of traffic signs as you drive.
- Make a timeline of things you have studied—pictures of your child since birth or pictures of when family members were born.
- Discuss taxes and how they are used.
- Visit a Thai restaurant and try something new.

Vocations: Tailor, taxi-cab driver, taxidermist, teacher, telemarketer, television anchor, therapist, travel agent

Books:
- *The Legend of the Teddy Bear* by Frank Murphy
- *Cranberry Thanksgiving* by Wende and Harry Devlin
- *The Finest Horse in Town* by Jacqueline Briggs Martin
- *Truman's Aunt Farm* by Jama Kim Rattigan
- *Three Names* by Patricia MacLachlan
- *They Were Strong and Good* by Alice and Robert Lawson

Music Appreciation:
Trombone playing. Watch on YouTube—boys playing a trumpet and girls playing a trumpet.

Composers:
Germaine Tailleferre 1892–1983, Piotr Ilyich Tchaikovsky 1840–1893, Georg Philipp Telemann 1681–1767

Hymn: "Turn Your Eyes Upon Jesus"

Songs: "I'm a Little Teapot," "Twinkle Twinkle Little Star," "There Was an Old Lady Who Swallowed a Fly," "There Was a Crooked Man"

Movies to Watch: *Tangled, Tarzan, Tinkerbell, Toy Story, Thomas the Train*

The Letter U

 Sound : /u/, /U/, /oo/ (us, unit, put)

 Kinesthetic: Form letters out of play-dough, your body, or make letters outside from nature (sticks, leaves, petals, pinecones, etc.).

 Alphabet Notebook
• **Block Letter Pages:** Make **u**nderwater **U**s by coloring blue and adding fish to your block letter U's page.

• **Clip Art Pages:** Make **u**nderwater **U**s by coloring blue and adding fish to your block letter U's page. Cut and paste clip art onto your **U**'s page.

Uu **Handwriting Pages:** Practice several upper and lower case letters every day this week.

 Menu Ideas:
Ugli fruit, **u**nagi (sushi), **u**nleavened bread, **u**nsweetened chocolate, **u**pside down cake, **U**tz™ chips, **U**s shaped out of cookie dough or pretzel dough, then bake.

 Field Trip Ideas:
Umpire's room (at a baseball field) or **u**niform store, **U**S Navy historical ships

 Bible Ideas:
unleavened bread, the **U**pper Room, **U**riah, **U**zziah

Copy Work & Memory Verse: "Unto Thee, O God, do we give thanks..." (Psalm 75:1).

Character Traits: **U**nselfish, **u**pright, **u**seful

Art:
• Make an **u**nderwater picture: Tissue paper for seaweed, construction paper for fish, etc. Use clear contact paper to keep it as a placemat.
• Make an **u**mbrella: With a black marker, draw a black dot in the center of a paper plate (for the tip). Draw a couple lines coming down from tip; then let child paint the **u**mbrella. You can glue yellow boot tips to peek out from bottom of umbrella. Or color an umbrella printable free on-line..
• Color a **u**nicorn.

Poetry:

Mother Goose:
UP THE WOODEN HILL TO BLANKET FAIR
Up the wooden hill to Blanket Fair,
What shall we have when we get there?
A bucket full of water,
And a pennyworth of hay,
Gee up, Dobbin, all the way!

Activities:
• Make and explain **u**nleavened bread.
• Bend pipe cleaners into "**U**" shapes.
• Go outside with your **u**mbrellas for sun or rain.
• Spin an **u**mbrella.
• Describe **u**niqueness.
• Hang **u**pside down.
• Walk **u**pstairs instead of using an elevator.
• Watch someone ride a **u**nicycle.
• Swim **u**nderwater (even in the bathtub).
• Teach child how to use **u**tensils properly.
• Teach child how to set the table with **u**tensils.
• Using a masking tape line (like a tightrope), walk with a small **u**mbrella like in the circus.
• Teach child to hold their breath **u**nderwater in tub or pool.
• Point out and discuss professions that wear **u**niforms (doctors, bus drivers, students, etc.) and why kids wear **u**niforms.
• **U**pside Down: Cut pictures from magazines and catalogs, and glue them onto a piece of paper **u**pside down.
• Throw a ball **u**nderhanded.
• Organize the **u**tensil drawer with your child.
• Instruct child how to **u**nlock a door with a key.
• Let your child pick out some new **u**nderwear.

Math Ideas:
- Describe a **u**nit of measurement.
- Discuss the symbol for **u**nequal.

Science Ideas:
- **U**nderwater animals—sea urchins
- **U**nderwater plants
- Investigate animals that live **u**nderground.
- Learn about **u**nicorns.
- Learn about **u**ltrasounds online—vet ultrasounds and watch baby grow ultrasounds.
- List ways we can go **up**—stairs, jumping, elevators, escalator, hot air balloons, airplanes, helicopters, space ships, climbing trees, etc.
- Study the **u**niverse.

Social Studies Ideas:
- The history of the **U**nited States.
- The history of the **U**nited States Dollar.
- Explain the differences in the **U.S.** Military (Army, Navy, Air Force, Marines, Coast Guard)
- Print out a free, printable USA flag online and color.
- Discuss **U**nited States population: 322,762,018
- Put together a **U**nited States map puzzle.
- Color a free on-line printable map of the **U**nited States.

Vocations: **U**mpire, **u**ndercover agent, **u**ndertaker, **u**pholsterer, **u**sher, **U.S.** Congressman

Books:
- *Uncle Wiggily's Storybook* by Howard Garis
- *Great Day For Up* by Dr. Seuss
- *The Ugly Duckling* by Hans Christian Anderson
- *The Umbrella Day* by Nancy Evans Cooney
- *The Favorite Uncle Remus* by Joel Chandler Harris
- *Umbrella* by Taro Yashima

Music Appreciation:
Ukelele Playing

Hymn: "Up From The Grave He Arose"

 Songs: "Under the Sea"

 Movies to Watch: *Up, Underdog*

Notes:

_____

_____

_____

_____

_____

_____

_____

_____

_____

The Letter V

 Sound : /v/ (van)

 Kinesthetic: Form letters out of play-dough, your body, or make letters outside from nature (sticks, leaves, petals, pinecones, etc.).

 Alphabet Notebook
• **Block Letter Pages:** Let your child cut out pictures of vegetables from a grocery flyer and paste onto your block letter **V**'s page.
Take strips of tissue paper and twist them to make vines. Glue the strips onto **V**s. You will need to make these tiny. Cut leaves out of green paper and glue around the vine.

• **Clip Art Pages:** Cut and paste clip art onto your **V**'s page.

V v **Handwriting Pages:** Practice several upper and lower case letters every day this week.

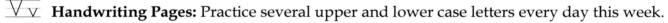

 Menu Ideas:
Valencia oranges, **V**alencia orange juice, **v**anilla ice-cream, **v**anilla pudding, **v**anilla wafers, **v**eal, **v**egetables, **v**eggie burger, **V**elveeta™ cheese, **v**enison, **v**ermicelli, **V**ienna roll, **V**ienna sausage, salt and **v**inegar chips, **v**inegar, **v**inaigrette, **v**itamins, **V**-8™

 Field Trip Ideas:
Ride in a **v**an; go to a **v**eterinary office; see a **v**oting booth; or participate in kid's **v**oting.

Bible Ideas:
Bible **v**erse: Find your child's favorite **v**erse and hang it up in their room.
Discuss a life **v**erse.

Copy Work & Memory Verse: "...Verily, verily, I say unto you, Whatsoever ye shall ask the Father in My name, He will give it you" (John 16:23).

Character Traits: Virtuous, visionary, vivacious

Art:
- Make a valentine for someone.
- Make veggie prints: Using potato, broccoli, or any other veggie. Cut, dip in paint, and stamp on paper.
- Make a vegetable collage using a grocery store insert.
- Paint a Bible verse on a wall. Or stick a verse on the wall using vinyl letters.

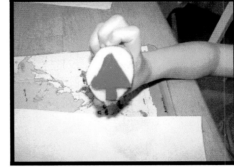

Artist Study:
- Leonardo da Vinci and discover the fascinating things he invented.
- Jan Vermeer

Poetry:

Mother Goose:
VINTERY, MINTERY, CUTERY, CORN
Vintery, mintery, cutery, corn,
Apple seed and apple thorn;
Wire, briar, limber lock,
Three geese in a flock.
One flew east,
And one flew west,
And one flew over the cuckoo's nest.

Activities:
- Play volleyball with a beach ball or volleyball.
- Teach child to vacuum their room.
- Host a Valentine's party.
- Learn about the history of Valentine's Day and St. Valentine.
- Make Valentine cookies.
- Look through a viewfinder.
- Make a veggie tray with carrots, broccoli, celery, etc., and include several dips for a snack.
- Taste real vanilla.
- Make a recipe with vanilla extract in it.
- Feel velvet.
- Buy something from a vending machine.
- Watch a ventriloquist.

• Have a **V-8**™ and smack yourself on the forehead like the commercial.
• Put flowers in a **v**ase for your child to enjoy.
• Distort **v**oice by speaking into an electric fan.
• **R**ecord **v**oice on tape or computer (high, low, whisper, squeaky, etc.).
• Describe a **v**illain. Watch a movie and point out the **v**illain.
• Taste **v**inegar.
• Grow a **v**egetable garden.
• Take pet to the **v**et.
• Make a **v**ideo of your child doing something special or of the family being silly. Send it to Americas Funniest Videos.
• **V**olunteer your time to someone who needs it.
• Take a **v**acation.
• Learn **v**owels.
• Show your child a picture of our **v**ice president.
• **V**itamins: Buy child some children's chewable **v**itamins. (Check with your doctor first.)
• Teach the meaning of a **v**egetarian. Be a **v**egetarian for a day.

Math Ideas:
• Draw **v**ertical lines. Teach **v**ertical vs. horizontal.
• Discuss **v**alue.
• Show a **v**ertex.

Science Ideas:
• Teach how to stop spreading **v**iruses by washing your hands and not touching your eyes, nose, or mouth.
• Drop **v**inegar tinted with food coloring onto a pan filled with baking soda. Fizzy fun!
• Make a homemade **v**olcano.
• Watch an active **v**olcano.
• Learn about **v**ultures.
• Discuss **v**omit.
• Grow or plan a **v**egetable garden.
• Study **V**enus.
• Discuss **v**enom. Google what snake **v**enom can do to blood.

Social Studies Ideas:
• Discover **v**olcano facts and where **v**olcanos are located around the world.
• Learn about the **V**andals and where our word "vandalize" comes from.
• Show your child **v**andalism in your town.
• Discuss ways you can **v**olunteer in your community.
• Discuss **v**alues.
• Learn about the **v**oting process.

Vocations: Vacuum cleaner salesperson, valet, ventriloquist, veterinarian, vice president, video game developer, videographer, violinist

Books:
- *The Velveteen Rabbit* by Margery Williams Bianco
- *Volcanoes: Mountains That Blow Their Tops* by Nicholas Nirgiotis
- *VeggieTales* Books
- *Children's Book of Virtues* by William J. Bennett
- *Very Last First Time* by Jan Andrews

Music Appreciation:
Listen to vocals (A capella) Be sure to tell child that this is pure vocals, no music at all. Listen to a violin sonata, vaudeville act, and vaudeville singing.

Composers:
Giuseppe Verdi 1813–1901, Antonio Vivaldi 1678–1741

Hymn: "Victory in Jesus"

Movies to Watch: Vintage *Mickey Mouse, Veggie Tales*

Notes:

_____

_____

_____

_____

_____

_____

_____

The Letter W

 Sound : /w/ (walk)

 Kinesthetic: Form letters out of play-dough, your body, or make letters outside from nature (sticks, leaves, petals, pinecones, etc.).

 Alphabet Notebook
• **Block Letter Pages:** Watercolor your block letter **W**s, or cut the letters out of black paper and draw a **w**eb with **w**hite chalk.

• **Clip Art Pages:** Cut and paste clip art onto your **W**'s page.

Handwriting Pages: Practice several upper and lower case letters every day this week.

 Menu Ideas:
Wafers, **w**affles, **W**aldorf salad, **w**alnuts, **w**ater chestnut, **w**atercress, **w**ater, **w**atermelon, **w**heat germ, **W**heaties™, **W**heat Thins™, mini **w**heats cereal, **w**hipped cream, **w**hite rice, **w**hole **w**heat bread, **w**hole **w**heat pasta, **w**ild rice

 Field Trip Ideas:
Go to a **W**al-Mart or on a **w**alking tour of historic town. See **w**aves. Go to a **w**ater park. See a **w**aterfall. Tour your local news station **W**_ _ _ . Meet a **w**eather forecaster, a **w**ood carver, or a **w**riter.

 Bible Ideas:
The **w**hale and Jonah's story, Jesus **w**alking on **w**ater, the **w**ise men, **w**itnessing, **w**orship

• **Missionaries:** **W**illiam Carey (1761–1834), India; **W**illiam Booth (1829–1912), England (Salvation Army)

Copy Work & Memory Verse: "What time I am afraid, I will trust in Thee" (Psalm 56:3).

Character Traits: Warm, willing, wise, witty

Art:
- Try paper weaving.
- Paint with watercolors.
- Make a magic wand.

- Draw a woman.
- Learn to whittle.
- Make your own whirligig.
- Try wire sculpting.
- Make a wind chime.
- Try woodworking. Some large hardware stores have free kids classes on Saturday mornings.

Artist Study: NC Wyeth

Poetry:
- Read William Wordsworth's poems online and on Ambleside's Online Poems of William Wordsworth

Mother Goose:

WEE WILLIE WINKIE

Wee Willie Winkie runs through the town,
Upstairs and downstairs, in his nightgown;
Rapping at the window, crying through the lock,
"Are the children in their beds? Now it's eight o'clock."

Activities:
- Pull child in a wagon.
- Wiggle.
- Explain the definition of a widow.
- Have your child look through your wedding pictures.

- Show your wedding ring to your child and tell the story.
- Blow a whistle.
- Attempt whistling. Listen to Andy Griffith's theme song.
- Try on a wig.
- Waddle like a duck.
- Splash water.
- Get wet.
- Do something special on Wednesday.
- Pull weeds with your child.

- Remind your child to say, "You're **w**elcome," when thanked.
- Have a **w**eenie roast.
- **W**hisper in your child's ear.
- Show your child a **w**eeping **w**illow.
- Have a **w**ater gun fight.
- **W**ade in **w**ater or put your feet in a **w**ading pool.
- Discover the **w**ater **w**ays in your area—lake, pond, creek, or river.
- Find a **w**elcome mat and **w**ipe your feet.
- Throw a penny in a **w**ishing **w**ell and make a **w**ish.
- **W**ash **w**indows together. Your child can use a squeegee. I have found they do better with this when they are little.
- **W**ash dishes together.
- Make your own all natural **w**hipped cream.
- Teach child how to **w**ash fruits and vegetables.
- Illustrate **w**hining for your child.
- Pour **w**ater using different containers—cups, plastic bottles, bowls, buckets, pitchers, etc.
- Buy a **w**hoopee cushion.
- Take a **w**alk together. Have your child describe the **w**alk and what she/he saw.
- Teach your child to **w**ink.
- Look at a map of the **w**orld.
- Chew **W**riggly™ gum.
- Go with a parent to "Take your child to **w**ork" day.
- Show your child a **w**ristwatch.
- Make a **w**ish.
- Talk to a **w**aiter or **w**aitress; ask if you can pray for them.
- Play **w**aiter **w**aitress and have child make a menu and help prepare and cook food. Create a menu (can be pictures colored in) the child can hold and check off when taking orders and waiting on "tables." Use family and dolls for customers and teach child to serve.

Math Ideas:
- Learn the days of the **w**eek.
- **W**eigh your child and **w**rite it down.
- Measure the **w**idth of objects.
- Try some **w**ord problems for preschoolers.

Science Ideas:
- Learn about **w**orms.
- Make your own **w**orm farm.
- Read about **w**hales, **w**olves, **w**alruses, or **w**hippoorwills.
- Study the **w**eather.
- Discuss **w**inter.
- Learn about **w**indmills: How **w**ind turbines work.
- Learn about how **w**ind is a powerful source of energy.
- Drink **w**ater. Discuss the benefits of **w**ater.

Social Studies Ideas:
- Discuss a **w**orld map: Show the continents.
- Print a **w**orld map free online and color.
- Read about George **W**ashington, **W**alt Disney, **W**illiam Shakespeare.
- Learn to **w**altz.
- Study briefly **WWI** or **WWII.**
- Learn how **W**ilbur and Orville **W**right discovered flight.

Vocations: **W**aiter, **w**aitress, **w**arden, **w**eatherman, **w**eaver, **w**ebsite developer, **w**ebmaster, **w**edding director, **w**oodcarver, **w**rangler, **w**inemaker, **w**riter

Books:
- *I Went Walking* by Sue Williams
- *Wings on Things* by Marc Brown
- *I Wish That I Had Duck Feet* by Theo LeSieg
- *Wacky Wednesday* by Theo LeSieg
- *Stories from Around the World* by Heather Amery
- *We're Going on a Bear Hunt* by Michael Rosen (see livepage.apple.com)
- *Who Owns the Sun?* by Stacy Chbosky

Music Appreciation:
Listen to and **w**atch a **w**altz online or in person. Listen to **WWI** and **WWII's** popular songs.

Composers:
Richard **W**agner 1813–1883, Carl Maria von **W**eber 1786–1826, John Williams (1932-)

Hymn: "**W**hat Child Is This?"

Songs:
"Who's Afraid of the Big Bad **W**olf"
"What a **W**onderful **W**orld"
"There's a **W**iggle in My Toe"
"He's Got the **W**hole **W**orld in His Hands"

Movies to Watch: *Wallace and Gromit, Wall-E, Many Adventures of Winnie the Pooh, Wreck It Ralph*

Notes:

The Letter X

 Sound : /ks/ (fox)

 Kinesthetic: Form letters out of play-dough, your body, or make letters outside from nature (sticks, leaves, petals, pinecones, etc.).

 Alphabet Notebook
- **Block Letter Pages:** Draw **X**s on your block letter **X**'s page. You could use chalk on black letters to look like bones.

- **Clip Art Pages:** Cut and paste clip art onto your **X**'s page.

X̲x̲ **Handwriting Pages:** Practice several upper and lower case letters every day this week.

 Menu Ideas:
Use different foods to create the shape of **X** on a plate such as pretzels, carrots, or celery sticks, **X** jello™ wigglers, **X**avier soup, **X**avier steak (American steak dish), **X** cookies, **x**om tum (very hot and spicy Thai dish), **X**-tra™ gum, **X**-treme™ candy

 Field Trip Ideas:
X-ray machine (at a hospital or lab). Look for a bo**x** car at a train station or going through town. Do something e**X**citing this week!

 Bible Ideas:
The crucifi**X**, e**X**altation, E**X**odus, Feli**X**, **X**erxes

- **Missionary:** St. Francis **X**avier (1506–1552), Asia

Copy Work & Memory Verse: "...E**X**ceeding great and precious promises are given unto us" (2 Peter 1:4).

Character Traits: E**X**cited, e**X**traordinary

Art:
- Put colored **X**s on a large letter **X** using yarn.
- Decorate a bo**x**.
- Decorate an inde**x** card.

• Ask an appliance store for a refrigerator or appliance bo**x**. Take home, decorate with paint or markers, and play!

• Make a butterfly out of an **X**.

Poetry:

Mother Goose:
X, Y, AND TUMBLEDOWN Z
X, Y, and tumbledown Z,
The cat's in the cupboard
And can't see me.

Activities:
- Play tic-tac-toe using **X**s and Os.
- Play large scale tic-tac-toe using sticks and paper plates for **X**s and Os and jumprope, hoses, and rope to make game board.
- Mi**X** together cookie dough or cake mi**X**.

• Use a real mi**X**er.

• Play in a sandbo**X** out in your yard or the park.

• Make a sandbo**X** out of a plastic storage container with a lid for inside fun. Include measuring cups.

• Light a beeswa**X** candle, or use beeswa**X** products.

• Burn a candle and watch the wa**X** melt.

• Play a song on a jukebo**X**.

• Put together a simple toolbo**X** for your child. Teach child to use a hammer, a nail, a screw, etc.

• Tell your child about chicken po**X**.

• Get the mail out of or drop mail into a mailbo**X**.

• Check your child's refle**X**es.

• E**X**hale to a count of si**X**.

• E**X**plain a hoa**X**.

• Ride in a ta**X**i.

• Fi**X** something with your child.

• Make a simple sewing bo**X** with a pin cushion, buttons, and cloth. Teach child to learn a simple sewing stitch.

• Go through your (or a grandmother's) sewing bo**X**.

• Make pi**X**ie dust (baking soda or baking soda and glitter), keep in an envelope, and sprinkle around child's bed to ward off bad dreams.

• Wa**X** your car with your child.

• Show child an ony**X** stone or image.

- Watch kickboXing techniques. Explore the history of kickboxing.
- Show child eXit signs in every commercial building you enter—store, library, bank, movie theater.
- Make **X**-shaped cookies.
- TeXt a friend. Help your child write/send a teXt to a friend or relative. Include a picture.
- Schedule your eXterminator to come this week.
- Show child an image or real phloX. Plant some. Paint some.
- FaX your dad (or other loved one) at work.
- Have child eXplain something they have learned this week.
- EXercise.
- Do a fun eXperiment.
- Illustrate an eXaggeration.
- Show a fire eXtinguisher and explain its uses. Spray one if you are able (parental supervision required).
- Get eXcited!
- Take child to their yearly doctor check-up eXamination.
- Watch an eXplosion on-line. (Explain the danger.)
- Teach child when to use an eXclamation point.
- Watch someone cut wood with an aXe. (Make sure to tell child the dangers of using an axe and to never pick one up without adult supervision.)
- Make a pirate map where **X** marks the spot for the treasure. Perhaps make a real map and count steps in each direction. You can make the map look authentic by using a woodburner on the edges and soaking the paper in tea water. Put a special surprise in the place where **X** marks the spot.

Math Ideas:
- Count to siX.
- Give child siX M&M'S™ or siX (6) candies.
- Write the number siX. Have child copy the word siX.
- Count by siXes—6, 12, 18, 24, 30, 36, 42, 48, 54, 60.
- Determine the number that comes neXt; plus one facts.
- Draw a heXagon.
- Define aXis (and show child what it is).

Science Ideas:
- Look at **X**-rays online or in a book. Show child a real **X**-ray. You can order yours for free if you have had any taken this year.
- Learn about x-ray fish.
- Learn about fish inside out with **X**-ray vision photos from the Smithsonian online.
- Read about foXes and oXen.
- Show eXamples of wheels and aXles.
- Learn about our galaXy.
- EXplain oXygen.
- Discover eXtinct animals.

Social Studies Ideas:
- Learn about TeXas
- Read about Xerxes the Great.
- Learn about famous eXplorers: Ferdinand Magellan, Neil Armstrong, Daniel Boone, etc.
- Tell your child about taXes—kinds of taXes and what they are used for in the community and government.

Vocations: eXterminator, X-ray technician, xylophone player, xylographer

Books:
- *Box Car Children* by Gertrude Chandler Warner
- *A Fox: The Sound of X* by Alice K. Flanagan
- *Fox in Socks* by Dr. Seuss
- *The Adventures of Taxi Dog* by Debra and Sal Barracca
- *The Taxi that Hurried* a Golden Book
- *Ox-Cart Man* by Donald Hall

Music Appreciation:
- Listen to a saXophone.
- Xoomii (khoomii, hoomii)—a type of Tuvan throat singing Mongolian throat singing.
- Listen to xylophone playing.

Hymn: "I EXhault Thee"

Songs: "SiX Little Ducks"

Movies to Watch: *The FoX and the Hound*

The Letter Y

 Sound : /y/, /i/, /I/ (yard, baby, my)

 Kinesthetic: Form letters out of play-dough, your body, or make letters outside from nature (sticks, leaves, petals, pinecones, etc.).

 Alphabet Notebook
* **Block Letter Pages:** Glue pieces of (yellow) yarn onto your block letter Y's page or paint the Ys with egg yolks.

* **Clip Art Pages:** Cut and paste clip art onto your Y's page.

Yy **Handwriting Pages:** Practice several upper and lower case letters every day this week.

 Menu Ideas:
Yams, yeast rolls, yellow food (scrambled eggs, yellow apples, yellow banana, yellow butter, yellow cake, yellow cheese, yellow corn, yellow pineapple, yellow rice, yellow squash), yogurt (try making homemade), yogurt-sicles (freeze fruit yogurt in popsicle containers. Use popsicle sticks for handles), yolk (egg yolk), Yoo-Hoo™, yucca

 Field Trip Ideas:
Visit a yarn shop. Go to a yard sale or have a yard sale. Meet a yodeler. Visit Yorktown (ask for a homeschooler discount).

 Bible Ideas:
Discuss how the word Yahweh sounds like your breathing. Discuss a yoke. "For my yoke is easy, and my burden is light" (Matthew 11:30).

Copy Work & Memory Verse: "Ye are the light of the world..." (Matthew 5:14).

Character Traits: Youthful

Art:
• **Y**olk painting: Mix paint with egg **y**olk and paint. The egg **y**olk makes paint shiny like a shellac. (Be sure to wash your hands.)

• Make something out of **y**arn.
• Make a **y**ellow collage from **y**ellow magazine pictures.
• **Y**arn crosses: Using **y**arn (**y**ellow if you have it), wrap around 2 popsicles sticks securing center to form a cross (†).

Poetry:

Mother Goose:
YOUNG ROGER AND DOLLY
Young Roger came tapping at Dolly's window,
Thumpaty, thumpaty, thump!

He asked for admittance; she answered him "No!"
Frumpaty, frumpaty, frump!

"No, no, Roger, no! as you came you may go!"
Stumpaty, stumpaty, stump!

Activities:
• Bake something with **y**east and watch it rise.
• Make your own **Y**oo-Hoo™
• Use **y**east to make bread.
• Play with a **y**o-**y**o.
• Learn how to throw a **y**o-**y**o.
• Watch professional **y**o-**y**oers on-line.
• Learn **y**o-**y**o tricks.
• Try some Christian **y**oga or Holy **Y**oga™ (strength and flexibility).
• When your child is excited, **y**ell, "**Y**ipee!"
• **Y**ell.
• Make or go out for something **y**ummy. Ask your child for ideas.
• See the world's largest **y**achts online.
• Discuss what the **y**ield sign means.
• Play in your **y**ard.
• Introduce your child to the **y**ellow pages and how it is organized alphabetically, residentially, and by business.
• Get your child to say **y**es. Say **y**es to your child this week too.
• Make **y**ellow play-dough.

• **Y**awn. See if you can make yourself **y**awn. See if you can make your dog **y**awn.

Math Ideas:
• Discuss a **y**ear—number of months, number of weeks, number of days. How old will child be on next birthday?
• Measure with a **y**ard stick.
• Measure your **y**ard.

Science Ideas:
• Read about **y**aks.
• Learn about the **y**ucca plant.
• Visit or watch a video about **Y**ellowstone National Park.
• **Y**ucky science experiments
• Discuss the science of **y**awning. Why do we **y**awn?
• Can you make it through a video of **y**awners without **y**awning?
• Make your own **y**ogurt.
• Make **y**ogurt popsicles.

Social Studies Ideas:
• Discuss the civil war. Who were the **Y**ankees?
• Learn about **Y**emen.
• What is a **y**uppy?

Vocations: **Y**achtsman, **y**arn maker, **y**east maker, **y**odeler, **y**outh pastor

Books:
• *Yellow Ball* by Molly Bang
• *Yard Sale* by Mitra Modarressi (order from library to view)
• *Little Blue and Little Yellow* by Leo Lionni
• *The Big Yawn* by Keith Faulkner
• *When I Was Young in the Mountains* by Cynthia Rylant
• *See the Yak Yak* by Charles Ghingna
• *The Yak Who Yelled Yuck* by Carol Pugliano-Martin

Music Appreciation:
Learn to **y**odel. Listen to a **y**odeler and attempt to imitate a **y**odel. Listen to **Y**anni.

Hymn: "Yesterday, Today, Forever"

 Songs: "Yankee Doodle," "Yellow Submarine" (Beatles)

 Movies to Watch: *Old Yeller, The Yearling* (1946)

Notes:

_____

_____

_____

_____

_____

_____

_____

_____

_____

_____

The Letter Z

  Sound : /z/ (zoo)

 Kinesthetic: Form letters out of play-dough, your body, or make letters outside from nature (sticks, leaves, petals, pinecones, etc.).

 Alphabet Notebook
• **Block Letter Pages:** Draw zig-zags on your block letter **Z**'s page or color your **Z**s with black and white stripes, like a zebra. Make a zipper rubbing on your **Z**s.

• **Clip Art Pages:** Cut and paste clip art onto your **Z**'s page.

Handwriting Pages: Practice several upper and lower case letters every day this week.

 Menu Ideas:
Zero™ candy bar, zero-shaped cereal (Cheerios™), Zesta™ crackers, zest of a lemon or orange, ziti, zoo Animal Crackers™, zucchini (fried), zucchini bread, Zwieback™ toast

 Field Trip Ideas:
Find a zeppelin (tour a blimp).Visit a zoo and see the zebras. (A great way to end the year!)

Bible Ideas:
Zaccheaus, Zachariah, Zacharias, Zephaniah, Zion, Zipporah,

Copy Work & Memory Verse: "Zion heard, and was glad..." (Psalm 97:8).

Character Traits: Zealous

Art:
- ZiplocTM bags: Mix colors in bags with paint—blue + yellow = green; red + blue = purple, etc.
- Draw a zebra.
- Create zectangles.
- Create a zebra toilet paper roll craft.
- Glue zig-zag rick rack in the shape of a 'Z' onto construction paper.

Poetry:

Mother Goose:
THE ALPHABET
A, B, C, and D,
Pray, playmates, agree.
E, F, and G,
Well, so it shall be.
J, K, and L,
In peace we will dwell.
M, N, and O,
To play let us go.
P, Q, R, and S,
Love may we possess.
W, X, and Y,
Will not quarrel or die.
Z, and ampersand,
Go to school at command.

Activities:
- Play zoom, zoom, zoom with tiny toy cars.
- Create zipper rubbings.
- Fry some zucchini.
- Have your child write the word "zero."
- Discuss zip codes. Have child memorize yours.
- Determine your child's zodiac symbols by month of birth.
- Teach child how to zip up coat with a zipper by him or herself.
- Walk in a zig-zag. (Use masking tape or show child what a zig-zag is on paper first.)
- Cut lots of zig-zag lines on paper. (Use parental supervision.)
- Look for zeros in signs, license plates, junk mail, and house numbers.
- Discover zeppelins.
- Plant zinnia seeds.

Math Ideas:
- Teach your child the zero facts: 1+0=1, 2+0=2, 3+0=3, etc.
- Teach zero and zillion. Write these numbers.

Science Ideas:
• **Z**oo animal guessing game: Pretend to be an animal and have child guess which one. Then guess while child acts out an animal.
• Learn about zebras.
• What is zoology?

Social Studies Ideas:
• Read about **Z**eus and the Greek Gods.
• Listen to Jim Weiss, Greek Myths.

Vocations: Zoo keeper, zoologist

Books:
• *Zella, Zack and Zodiac* by Bill Peet
• *If I Ran the Zoo* by Dr. Seuss
• *Put Me in the Zoo* by Robert Lopshire
• *The Zebra-Striped Whale with the Polka Dot Tail* by Shari F. Donahue
• *Zoom! Zoom! Zoom! I'm Off to the Moon* by Dan Yaccarino

Music Appreciation:
Learn about **Z**ither Music. Listen to **Z**ither Music.

Hymn: "Zion's Hill"

Songs: "Zip A Dee Do Dah"

Movies to Watch: *WiZard of OZ, OZ The Great and Powerful* (could be scary for some children), *Zootopia*

Alphabet Smash

Clip Art Pages

by Christina Parker Brown

Introduction

These A-Z clip art pages are meant to compliment the *Alphabet Smash* curriculum. Cutting and pasting will improve your child's dexterity and confidence as they build an Alphabet Notebook using copies of these clip art pages. They can also be downloaded for free at http://akahomeschoolmom.com/alphabet-smash-freebies. Pictures are best copied or printed in color but black and white will work too. Your child may use crayons, pencils, or markers to add color.

The *Alphabet Smash* Notebook that your child creates, is a portfolio that combines all things included in this *Alphabet Smash* book that you will do with your child or that your child achieves independently. It is a wonderful keepsake and can record what your child accomplished for the year.

Teach children to cut out the clip art pictures included in this book, found in magazines and discarded books themselves. Then paste them onto the letter page in their Alphabet Notebook. Don't worry about perfection. Allow your children to take ownership of their work. Allow them to make mistakes and to enjoy the process and the sense of accomplishment in the successes. I found it fun to get magazines like *Ranger Rick* or *National Geographic* for kids to add extra pictures they find to their alphabet pages. Once we even taped a preserved ant to the "A" page, traced and painted fingernails with real polish for the "F" page, and a put a lock of hair on the "H" page. Be creative. Keep these in the child's alphabet notebook for each letter. Remember to have fun.

May the Lord richly bless you as you teach your children!

Let the

Alphabet Smash

begin!

Aa

Bb

Cc

Dd

Ee

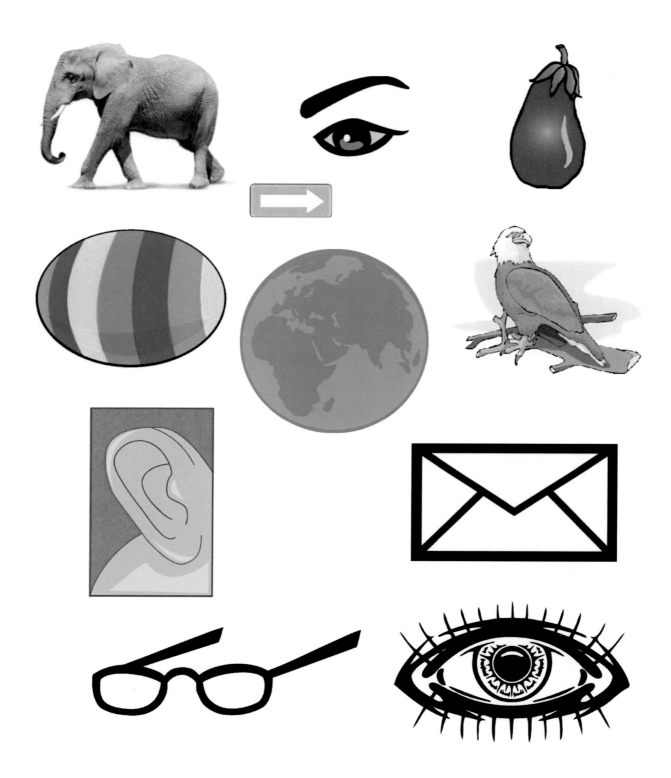

Ff

Gg

Hh

Ii

Jj

Kk

Ll

Mm

Nn

Oo

Pp

Qq

BE QUIET!

Quiver

"Quotation marks"

Rr

Ss

Tt

Uu

Vv

Ww

Xx

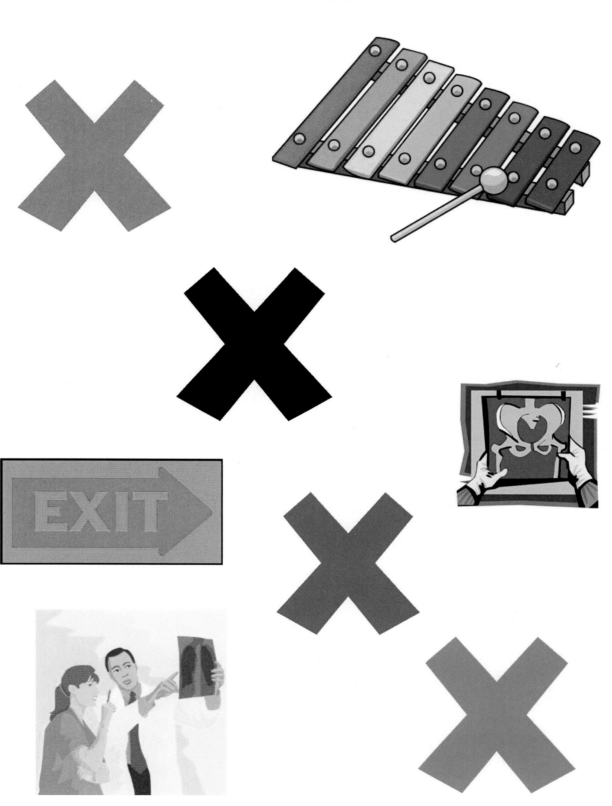

Yy

Zz

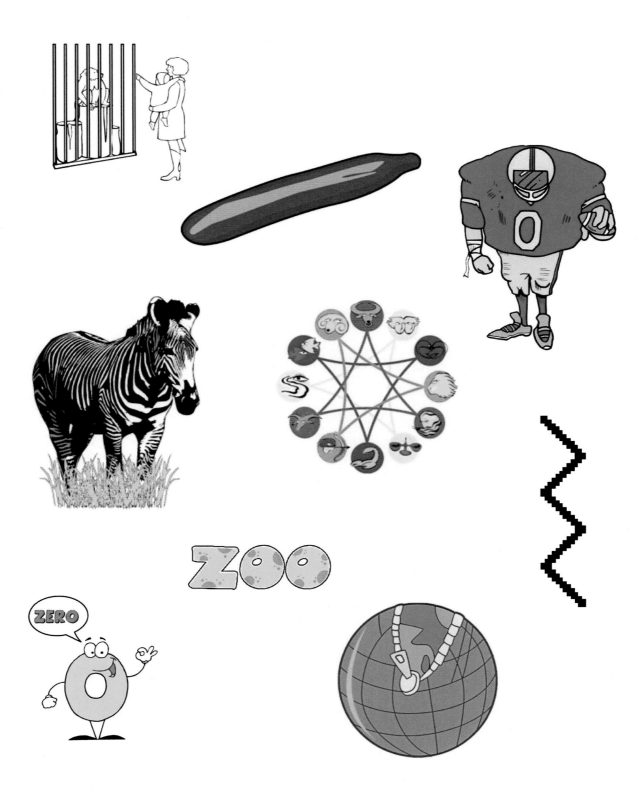

NOTES AND RESOURCES

Cowling, Douglas, Jeremy Irons, Wolfgang Amadeus Mozart, Peter Ilich Tchaikovsky, and George Frideric Handel. *The Classical Kids Collection. Tales of Enchantment and Classical Music*. Classical Kids, 1999. CD.

Lambert, Jane Claire. *Five in a Row*. Grandview, MO: Five in a Row Pub., 1997. Print.

Martin, Mildred A., and Edith Burkholder. *Missionary Stories with the Millers*. Minerva, OH: Green Pastures, 1993. Print.

Mason, Charlotte M. *An Essay towards Philosophy of Education*.: Kegan Paul, Trenchm Trubner, and Ltd, London , England, 1925. Republished by Tyndale House, Carol Stream, IL, 1989. Print.

Home Education. Vol. 1.: Kegan Paul, Trenchm Trubner, and Ltd, London , England, 1925. Republished by Tyndale House, Carol Stream, IL, 1989. Print.

Sherwood, Elizabeth A., Robert A. Williams, and Robert E. Rockwell. *More Mudpies to Magnets: Science for Young Children*. Mt. Rainier, MD: Gryphon House, 1990. Print.

Williams, Robert A., and Robert E. Rockwell. *Mudpies to Magnets*. First ed. N.p.: Gryphon House, 1987. Web.

Williams, Robert A., Robert E. Rockwell, and Elizabeth A. Sherwood. *Mudpies to Magnets: A Preschool Science Curriculum*. Mt. Rainier, MD: Gryphon House, 1987. Print.

Various. "Project Gutenberg's Mother Goose or the Old Nursery Rhymes." *The Project Gutenburg*. Anne Storer, 10 Dec. 2007. Web. 2 Sept. 2015.

PHOTO CREDITS:

All photographs (unless otherwise stated) taken by Christina Parker Brown.
Images used in this book are licensed and © Graphics Factory.com

COVER DESIGN:

Angela Waye of Haywire Media. www.AngelaWaye.com

AUTHOR PHOTOGRAPH:

Lindy Sellers http:\\lindysellers.com

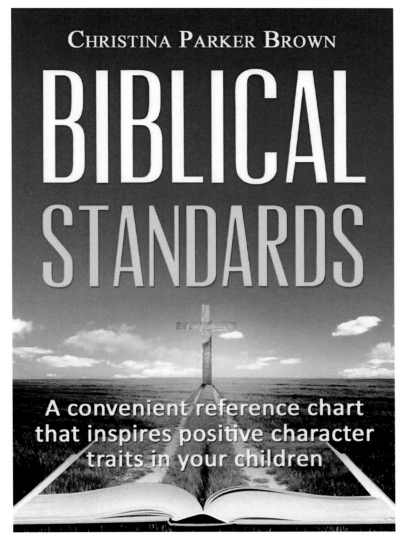

FREE DOWNLOAD

Discover Bible verses that go along with character traits you are training in your children!

Sign up for the author's newsletter and get a free copy of Biblical Standards: A convenient reference chart that inspires positive character traits in your children.

Get started at : http://akahomeschoolmom.com/lp-biblical-standards

Get the Kindle version at: https://www.amazon.com/Alphabet-Smash-Your-Childs-Adventure-ebook/dp/B01I8RTXQ8

ABOUT THE AUTHOR

Christina Parker Brown is a homeschool momma of three since 2000 and the author of AKAHomeschoolMom.com and *Alphabet Smash*. Her work has been featured in *Proverbs 31* magazine, *The Old Schoolhouse* magazine, *Home Educator Family Times*, *Greenhouse*, and others. Christina's passion is to encourage others to intentionally connect faith, family, and fun. She is a hopeless logophile and always brakes for yard sales. Her writing is inspired from her faith in Jesus Christ, adventures in NC with her Adventure Group, and her 24-year marriage to best friend, Richard.

You can connect with Christina at www.AKAhomeschoolmom.com, Facebook, Instagram, Twitter, and Pinterest.

Thank you for *Alphabet Smash*ing your way through this book! It is my hope that *Alphabet Smash* brought you memories, encouraged cuddling, and opened up the many wonders of God's love for us through His amazing creation.

If this book has been helpful to you, would you take a minute to let others know about how it has benefitted you and your children? Simply review *Alphabet Smash* on amazon.com or with whomever you purchased it. Tell whether you found it useful, what you loved about it, and even what needs improvement. Feedback helps me to become a better writer and can bless future *Alphabet Smash* teachers. It just takes a couple minutes!

Please share your thoughts about *Alphabet Smash* through social media, by email, or consider posting a positive review on Amazon.

Seriously grateful for your time,
Christina Parker Brown